PUB W

—————IN—————

The Malvern Hills

Roy Woodcock

COUNTRYSIDE BOOKS

NEWBURY, BERKSHIRE

COUNTRYSIDE BOOKS
3 Catherine Road
Newbury, Berkshire

To view our complete range of books,
please visit us at
www.countrysidebooks.co.uk

ISBN 1 85306 788 1

Designed by Graham Whiteman
Maps and photographs by the author
Cover photo supplied by Bill Meadows

Produced through MRM Associates Ltd., Reading
Typeset by Mac Style Ltd, Scarborough, N. Yorkshire
Printed by Woolnough Bookbinding Ltd., Irthlingborough

Contents

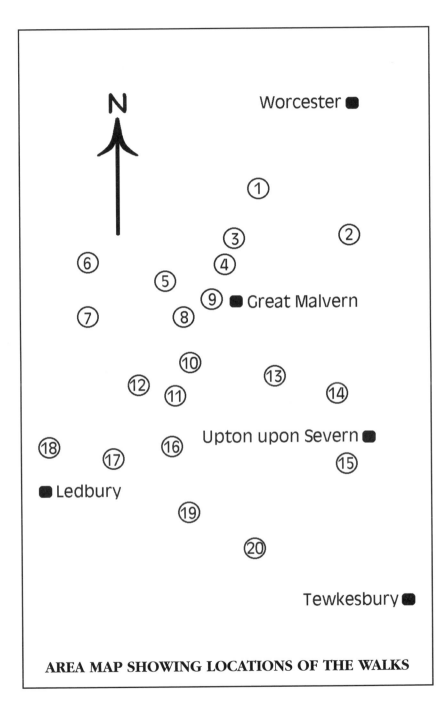

N

Worcester ■

①

②

③

④

⑥

⑤

⑨ ■ Great Malvern

⑦

⑧

⑩

⑫

⑬

⑪

⑭

⑱

⑯ Upton upon Severn ■

⑰

⑮

■ Ledbury

⑲

⑳

Tewkesbury ■

AREA MAP SHOWING LOCATIONS OF THE WALKS

PUBLISHER'S NOTE

We hope that you obtain considerable enjoyment from this book; great care has been taken in its preparation. However, changes of landlord and actual closures are sadly not uncommon. Likewise, although at the time of publication all routes followed public rights of way or permitted paths, diversion orders can be made and permissions withdrawn.

We cannot, of course, be held responsible for such diversion orders and any inaccuracies in the text which might result from these or any other changes to the routes nor any damage which might result from walkers trespassing on private property. We are anxious though that all details covering the walks and the pubs are kept up to date and would therefore welcome information from readers which would be relevant to future editions.

The sketch maps accompanying each walk are not always to scale and are intended to guide you to the starting point and give a simple but accurate idea of the route to be taken. For those who like the benefit of detailed maps, we recommend that you arm yourself with the relevant Ordnance Survey map in the Explorer series.

INTRODUCTION

Popular since Victorian times, and never more so than the present day, the narrow ridge of the Malverns is one of Britain's most recognisable landscapes. The silhouette seen from the east when driving on the M5, or looking out from the edge of the Cotswolds, can be as addictive as a drug, luring you back. Walkers, whether locals or visitors, love the unforgettable views both to and from the Malvern Hills. Pleasure, exercise and fresh air are all part of a walk on the hills.

The Malverns are both a range of hills and a cluster of settlements. The settlements (West Malvern, North Malvern, Malvern Link, Great Malvern, The Wyche, Malvern Wells, Little Malvern, Newland and Barnard's Green) have grown on the flanks of the hills and have gradually merged with each other and spread on to the flatter land. The centre is in Great Malvern which dates from 1085 when the Benedictine Priory was built. Growth was slow until 1842 when the Water Cure began and Doctors Wilson and Gully arrived to turn the village into a bustling spa town. Later in the 19th century the creation of schools (Boys' College in 1865, and Girls' College in 1893) encouraged further expansion. World War II brought another period of growth when the Radar Research Establishment moved to Malvern. This governmental research centre has remained here ever since, although its name has changed several times.

Building has never been easy in Malvern because of the steepness of the famous hills – the result of the rocks which form them. The hardness of the rocks is responsible for the fact that the hills stand up so prominently above the surrounding landscape. These old rocks have been dated at between 800 and 1,000 million years ago, though in some places they are a mere 600 million, but are all part of the Pre-Cambrian era. Great upheavals about 300 million years ago caused many major faults, as at The Wyche and The Gullet. To the west of the hills is the undulating landscape of the Silurian rocks, which were formed on the seabed 400 million years ago, but then uplifted and folded to create the undulating landscape with small, and often steep, hills, separated by green valleys. To the east of the hills the landscape is much younger geologically (250 million years), consisting of sands and clays from the Permo-Triassic period, a time of desert conditions.

Steep slopes are a feature of the range and this narrow ridge is noted for stiff climbs, characteristic of much larger hill masses than the Malverns. But there are also many gentle and fairly level paths too, starting from the car parks which have been provided, often in old quarries, by the Malvern Hills Conservators. Many of the main paths are gravelled and well drained – so this is a good walking area even in wet weather.

The county boundary runs along the top of the ridge in places, and the ridge top is followed by the Shire Ditch (Red Earl's Dyke). The ditch can be recognised in many of the walks, and it dates from 1287. After an argument over land and hunting rights, between Gilbert de Clare, the 3rd Earl of Gloucester, and Thomas de Cantiloupe, the Bishop of Hereford, a trench and bank was built by the Earl. It was designed to allow the Bishop's deer to leap over the ditch on to the Earl's land, but prevented deer from going in the opposite direction.

The undulating ridge consists of nine hilltops plus subsidiary summits, and most of the summits are fairly bare, being vegetated by grass. In the days when hundreds of sheep grazed here, larger areas of the hillsides were grassy too, but as the grazing declined in the 1960s and 1970s, for economic reasons, the trees, scrub and bracken have gradually spread up the hillside and threaten to take over.

Very important and influential to the hills are the Malvern Hills Conservators. Founded in 1884, and now consisting of both elected and nominated members, it was the loss of common land, remnants of the Malvern Chase, which really led to their formation. The MHC had their origin in a need to preserve the remaining common land, and manage it both for local residents and also for visitors. The other aims of the Conservators included stopping the quarrying, which was reaching the top of the ridge and would have destroyed the skyline. Quarrying was a major source of income for the area, but gradually the quarries were closed, the last being in 1977. The Conservators provide information for visitors including a set of three maps on a 1:10,000 scale. Amongst their responsibilities the Conservators are required by law to maintain the hills and surrounding commons for public access and recreation. This gives true freedom to roam.

As the hills have been designated a Site of Special Scientific Interest (SSSI), and the hills and commons are part of the Malvern Hills Area of Outstanding Natural Beauty, the Conservators work hand in hand with other organisations to make this one of the most cared for landscapes in Britain.

There is a lifetime of walking in these hills, and this collection of twenty circular routes is designed to whet your appetite for more. My choices are all based on the location of an interesting pub as a starting point. Each establishment provides good food and drink and they have a variety of histories – some are on old stagecoach or drovers' routes, others are situated in villages and others in the town or on the hillside, dependent on the visitors coming to the Malvern area. In each circuit, the walk will have views from the hills across the neighbouring lowlands to distant hills, or views from the lowlands looking at the line of the hills – and in some cases both. The routes range from just over a mile to 7 miles and all are easy to follow. Numbered paragraphs relate to points on the accompanying sketch map, but for added interest you may wish to take the relevant Ordnance Survey Explorer map (1:25,000) with you. The shorter routes are all suitable for a family or simply a leisurely stroll after (or before) a good lunch in the pub. The longer routes include a splendid trip to the top of the Herefordshire Beacon and one to the wonderful viewpoint of Midsummer Hill. Parking is possible at all the pubs, but do please ask permission to leave your car while you walk. Alternative parking spaces are often available.

So, put on your walking boots and prepare to be enchanted by this remarkable range of hills.

Roy Woodcock

① Collett's Green
The Three Nuns

Set in glorious countryside with views all round, we walk from the higher ground near the pub down to the meandering River Teme. Here we reach the ancient Powick Bridge, a famous battle site of the Civil War. The tall tower is a relic of the first hydro electric power station in England. To return to the starting point we cross the floodplain meadows, called hams, before facing the gentle climb back up from the flat river valley to pass over fields and along country lanes.

The small village of Collett's Green grew along the old Malvern road and is now adjacent to the A449 Worcester–Malvern road. This is a popular residential area and on this walk we pass many attractive old houses among the more modern development.

The impressive pub sign at the Three Nuns depicts the eponymous ladies luring customers into this delightful hostelry. A Marston's house, now part of the Wolverhampton and Dudley group, it offers a good selection of beers or you might prefer a local cider.

First rate home-cooked food is available, ranging from baguettes or toasted sandwiches up to very large meals if you are hungry walkers. Home-cured ham with chips or home-made spaghetti Bolognese are amongst the temptations. For relaxation a game of darts or a mind-bending attempt at solitaire might detain you after your meal. Food is served daily from 12 noon to 2 pm (3 pm on Sundays) and in the evening on Tuesday to Saturday from 6 pm to 11 pm. The large sheltered garden has a children's play area. Telephone: 01905 830442.

- **HOW TO GET THERE:** Take the A449 Worcester–Malvern road. Coming from Worcester, after 2 miles turn right at the cross-roads where there are traffic lights. From Malvern, turn left at the first lights reached 3 miles from Malvern.
- **PARKING:** There is off road parking alongside the pub.
- **LENGTH OF THE WALK:** $4\frac{1}{2}$ miles. Map: OS Explorer 204 Worcester and Droitwich Spa (GR 817514).

THE WALK

1. Leave the pub and turn left along the road between houses with neat and colourful gardens. Soon joined by a larger road, you follow the sign to Bransford. When the road divides take the left fork, still towards Bransford. After nearly 200 yards, where the road bends left, go right at the footpath sign. The drive alongside Woodman's Cottage yields superb views along the Malvern ridge. Pass one more house and go over a stile, with Lord's Wood to the right – carpeted with bluebells in spring. At the end of this field reach a stile and go on into the woods. Drop down to a stile and cross a small valley, then go up a few steps. Turn left to follow the clear path, with a track and small stream to your left. Leave the woods over a stile and walk along the edge of an open field to reach the track close to the river.

2. Turn right here (although if you need a rest there is a bench overlooking the river, a few yards to the left). Follow the river bank, but as this bends left keep straight ahead, moving away from the river. A hedge is now on your left, and a huge open field to your right. Reach a stile and keep straight on, with a line of trees on your left, but after about 40 yards when this field boundary turns left, rejoin the river bank. Follow the river as it slowly meanders downstream, on its way to meet the Severn. Try to spot the house with tall chimneys protruding above the trees at the top of the valley margin to the right. This is Ham Hill House, for a few years the home of Lord Lonsdale,

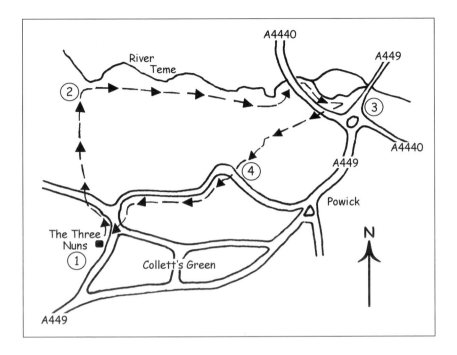

Marquis of Queensbury. At the end of this field you have to move 30-40 yards away from the river to find twin stiles and a footbridge – and a notice to say 'Private Fishing for St John's A.S'. Return to the river bank, and walk on towards the tall chimney at Powick Bridge. Reach another stile at the end of the next field and continue along the river bank. Keep your eyes open on the river for the interesting bird life, including kingfishers. I hope you will be as lucky as I certainly was on my last walk along this stretch – glimpsing a blue flash ahead of me. A ring of willow trees around the field to the right marks the location of a former meander – and there are plenty of trees growing alongside the present river too – hanging gracefully over the water. Reach another stile and walk through a jungle of Himalayan balsam to reach an underpass, where the noise of traffic will take over from the peace and solitude of the river bank. Once through the underpass, turn right, to pass the weir to join a track between the river and the road. Note the underpass to the right, which is the return route to the Three Nuns, but first, we are going to visit the 15th century bridge.

Turn left at a footpath sign, to continue along the river bank path. At the wooden gate go on to a narrow road, the former main road, where you turn left to visit the old bridge – no longer used for traffic, but having a remarkable history dating back to the Civil War. A plaque records: 'Powick Bridge River Teme. During the English Civil Wars between the Royalists and the Parliamentarians the First Skirmish on 23rd 9th 1642, and the last major battle 3rd 9th 1651 took place on or near this historic bridge'. The tall tower and mill were formerly a hydro electric power station, the first in Britain. The mill has been converted into luxury flats.

3. From the bridge, retrace your steps along the old road to the wooden gate, then turn right to walk alongside the River Teme on the right, with traffic over to the left. Before reaching the weir, an arrow points left to the underpass beneath the main road – A4440 – towards a pylon on the other side of the road. Cross a track, go through the fence and beneath the underpass to a stile. Once over this stile head across the huge field, one of the hams, following the direction of the arrow. In the far hedge, at the foot of the steep slope, and about 100 yards to the left of the lone house, reach a stile by a gate. Go over this and on up the valley margin, with a fence on the right. Wooden steps have been used to improve this path and make the climb easier. At the top turn left. Climb up to a stile, and continue along the clear path, with a fence and hedge to the right, and a steep slope down to the left. Pass a seat from where there are good views to the Powick chimney, and to Worcester Cathedral.

Where the path divides take the right turn over a stile, go up a few more steps and continue along the left margin of the field. After about 60-70 yards head across the field to the stile in the far right corner. You are now at the top of the climb, and views ahead open up to reveal the Malvern Hills.

4. Once over the stile with its smart doggy opening, you are on the bend of a narrow country lane and you go straight ahead, between hedges laden with blackberries and other fruits in season. As you walk there will often be no sound other than rooks cawing and swallows and house martins twittering overhead. Pass the timber-framed Collett's Green Farm with its old oast houses, and reach a T-junction. Turn left, retracing your steps towards the pub. After about 100 yards the road splits and the right fork leads you back to the Three Nuns.

2 Callow End
The Old Bush

The name Callow is derived from the Saxon word 'calwe', meaning bare hillside. Our walk takes us on to the Old Hills, still open and treeless in places, as well as across fertile and productive farm fields. Enjoy the all-round views throughout the year, and in summer do look out for the flowers, birds and butterflies which make the hills so marvellous for walkers and picnickers.

Callow End began as a linear settlement along the main road, but has grown to the east with a triangular patch of housing down Ferry Lane – which leads to a former crossing point of the Severn. Several old houses have survived along the road, and near the small green is the village shop, with the school, village hall and social club nearby. The small brick-built church of St James, with a bell turret, is a chapel of ease to Powick church – built in 1888. The outstanding building in the village is Stanbrook Abbey, a Benedictine nunnery founded at Cambrai in 1625. After expulsion from France in 1808, the nuns came to England and arrived at Stanbrook in 1838. The red

13

brick monastery buildings with the very imposing and distinctive tower date from the 1870s. The architect was E.W. Pugin, son of the Pugin who designed the houses of Parliament.

With fields at the back, a farm alongside and views to Stanbrook Abbey, the Old Bush is in a truly rural setting, and this is enhanced by the attractive garden and hanging baskets. The original 19th century building is quite small, and an outside wall faces you as you go in through the door. Extensions at the rear have provided room for a restaurant – and a deceptive amount of space for tables. A choice of Banks's and Marston's ales are there to tempt, with Pedigree being particularly popular. An extensive menu offers snacks, baguettes and full scale meals, with a delicious selection of starters and sweets. Food is served every day; from 12 noon to 2 pm on Mondays to Thursdays, till 2.30 pm on Fridays and 3 pm on Saturdays and Sundays; evening times are from 6 pm to 9 pm (8 pm on Sundays). Telephone: 01905 830792.

- **HOW TO GET THERE:** From Worcester, take the A449 Malvern road and turn left at Powick along the B4424 towards Upton. The Old Bush is at Callow End, on the right hand side of the main road.
- **PARKING:** The pub has a large parking area.
- **LENGTH OF THE WALK:** 3 miles. Map: OS Explorer 190 Malvern Hills and Bredon Hill (GR 834494).

THE WALK

1. From the car park, go back to the road and turn right for 30 yards and then right along Bush Lane. This narrow surfaced road leads between a few houses and passes the St George's Brewery located in the Old Bakehouse. This produces a variety of ales that are available in several of the local pubs and very popular with local drinkers. Continue along the lane, as the road deteriorates into a stone and gravel track. Beyond the final two houses, go through the gate onto the common.

Walk straight on, following the line of telegraph poles. The route stays close to the edge of the common, with fields to the right and the hills sloping up on the left. Keep straight on to a gate and stile, where a track goes on beyond, and a path is signed to the right. Go left here for about 20 yards to reach a stile. Climb up the steps and going over this stile brings the Malvern Hills into view. Walk along

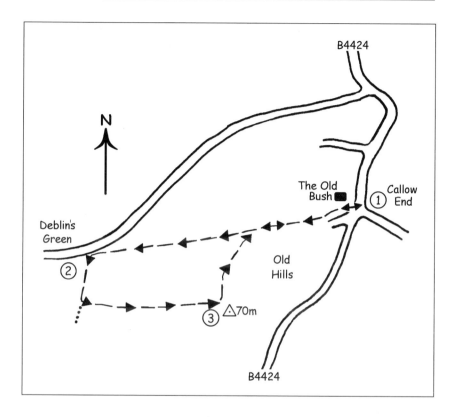

the right margin of the open grassy area, with a hedge on the right – and the track just referred to on the other side of the hedge.

At the end of this open area, the edge of the common, reach a gate and a stile. Continue, ignoring the path going left, and keep straight ahead along the right margin of the field. At the end of this field go right, through the gate and immediately turn left to a gate leading to a narrow path between gardens. Admire the colourful shrubs and flowers in the garden on the right and follow the path to an iron gate and onto a stony drive. There is a road a few yards to the right.

2. Turn left towards Upper Woodsfield Farm. As you walk along this drive, the views left to the Old Hills are quite impressive, but over to the right are the Malverns! The buildings of North Malvern are clear on the hillside and behind them the old quarries on the right side of North Hill. Sugar Loaf Hill and then the Worcestershire Beacon, the highest point on the range, are the next hills to the left.

Before reaching the farm buildings, ignore a footpath going right. Instead, turn left at the bridleway sign, through the iron gate and into a field, with a hedge on the left - heading back to the Old Hills. At the end of this field is a gate and you go straight on, with the field boundary now on the right - no hedge now, just a fence and occasional trees. The path may be pitted by horses' hooves, so watch where you are putting your feet. You are in the midst of a very green and rural landscape, with a lone house over to the left, and some farm buildings ahead and up to the left.

In the far right corner of this field, pass a small pond on the right and reach a wooden gate, beyond which is the Common. It is often muddy around this gate - because of horses' hooves; the Old Hills are very popular with riders. Follow the broad grassy path straight ahead, passing over two cross paths. Begin to climb, through an area with trees and bushes as well as grasses. At the top, the triangulation point (70m) is to your right.

3. Turn left to pass the benches and follow the edge of the grass, with trees on your left. When this small wooded area bends left, and the land slopes down, notice the clear views to the hills over to the left. Straight ahead in the distance is the building development on the site of the former Powick hospital, with Abberley Hill beyond. The route bends slightly right to descend from the open grassy area, through bushes and small trees, heading down one of several paths towards the buildings of Callow End. As you descend, aim for the edge of the common on your right, to reach a small glade with large old oak trees. Then rejoin the line of telegraph poles, where you turn right to walk off the common and retrace your steps along Bush Lane.

③ Newland
The Swan Inn

Starting from the ancient Swan Inn at Newland, this level walk, mostly over fields, follows the urban fringe of Malvern and gives clear and dramatic views of the northern edge of the Malvern Hills. You will be able to see how quarrying had been eating away at the ridge until prevented by the Malvern Hills Conservators, the earliest conservation organisation in Britain. The circuit ends on Newland's attractive green.

Newland now merges with Malvern, but retains its large green, with the church and almshouses on one side and the Swan across the road. The remarkable church of St Leonard and the almshouses (for their retired agricultural workers) were built by the Beauchamp family from nearby Madresfield in the 1860s. The highly decorated walls and roof make St Leonard's very cheery and colourful.

The Swan pub is mentioned in the Domesday Book and was formerly a coaching inn and a location where horses could be changed after a tiring journey from Worcester or Droitwich, also a halt for the horses and carts carrying salt across the hills into Herefordshire. The pub sign shows a captive swan, possibly because the Madresfield Estate, which still owns the pub, had royal permission to keep swans. The long bar has exposed beams and is decorated with hops, brasses and old prints. Bitters include Hobsons, Hook Norton and Shepherd Neame Spitfire, and Weston ciders are also popular here. The extensive menu offers snacks or meals in the bar, and the delightful restaurant in the next room has a wide menu, with oriental food a speciality. Business account customers come here for lunch, but walkers are also welcome and cricket lovers could watch a game on the neighbouring pitch on match days. Food is available from 12 noon to 2 pm and 7pm to 9 pm on Monday to Saturday. A traditional Sunday lunch is served, but there is no food on Sunday evenings. Telephone 01886 832224.

- **HOW TO GET THERE:** Newland is on the main Worcester-Malvern road, the A449, nearly 2 miles from Great Malvern.
- **PARKING:** There is a large car parking area at the pub, on the edge of the common.
- **LENGTH OF THE WALK:** $2\frac{1}{2}$ miles. Map: OS Explorer 190 Malvern Hills and Bredon Hill (GR 796490).

THE WALK

1. Walk along the left side of the Swan, passing the sign for Newland Cricket Club - and follow the track. A small pond is on the left, and at the cricket ground the pavilion is just to the right. Stay on the boundary at the left side of the field, to reach a kissing gate and continue along the left margin of the next field, passing another small pond. Go through a gap in the hedge into a large field. The hills are clear ahead now, with the lines of buildings about halfway up the incline. Big white houses from Victorian times are especially clear, and the Tank Clock Tower shows up prominently, below the quarries. Keep straight ahead, to cross this large field, or follow the left margin where the hedge turns left and then right, but you are heading to the far left corner of the field, aiming to the right of the houses. Reach a gateway in the corner of the field. Go through the gate and turn right (to the left is a parking/turning area for the houses).

2. Follow the clear path, with a hedge to the right and rough ground to the left with houses across the other side of this open space. When this path reaches houses, and continues to the right, close to the hedge, turn left here and walk on. Soon reach a narrow

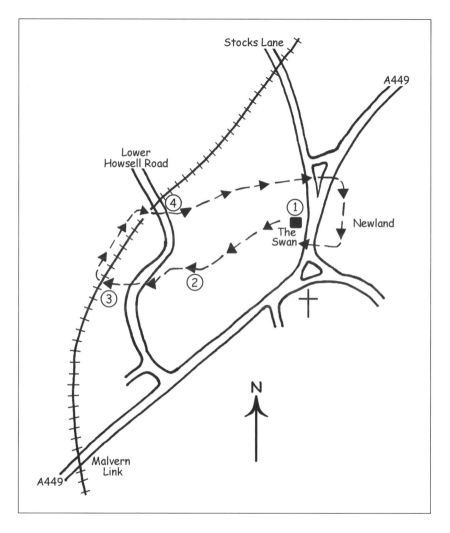

surfaced path and turn right, to walk through to Lower Howsell Road. Turn left opposite the New Inn.

3. After about 100 yards and just before reaching an immaculate thatched cottage (Summerfield Cottage), turn right onto the playing field, following the footpath sign. Pass the children's playground and follow the left margin of the field to reach a stile. Cross the railway, with great care, to another stile, then look left to enjoy the views to the hills. After the second stile, turn right along the field margin and walk parallel to the railway. At the end of this long field, the path

19

divides and you fork right to go up to the road. Turn right to cross over the bridge with good views along this very straight railway line in both directions. This stretch of railway is clearly seen in Walk 4. Walk on down the road for about 100 yards. Just before reaching two houses on the left, Elms Farm and Cider House – evidence of former use – turn left.

4. Go through the old iron gate and alongside the garden, and when this ends keep straight ahead across a large field. There are more good views from here, looking back at the ridge, stretching away to the south. See how the quarries nearly reached the top of the hill. Come alongside a hedge on the right, and then reach a gate at the end of this large field and bear slightly right along the line of a track. Follow the right margin of the next field, with the cricket ground just over the hedge. This track leads alongside a garden, to a large gate – and a gap through which you can go to the road, Stocks Lane. Turn right back to the pub, or go straight across onto a patch of grass, with an assortment of wild flowers (a carpet of snowdrops in season) and a variety of old well-established trees – oak, horse chestnut and poplar. Across the main road is the common and a circuit round the far side will take you past the church and the almshouses. If you want to visit the church, cross to the far side of the green near the hedge, and turn right towards the church. Then turn right again to cross the road and right along the pavement to complete the route back to the Swan.

④ Malvern
The Nag's Head

This exhilarating walk takes us on a stiff climb around North Hill to enjoy stunning views over this unique landscape, with a chance to visit Ivy Scar Rocks, the largest natural rocky outcrop on the Malverns.

The walk is at the northern end of the Malvern ridge. Quarrying was an important local industry here right up until 1960. You will see that many buildings are of local stone, and there are parallel rows of houses that cling to the steep slope, making a setting that is almost Alpine in appearance.

Situated close to the foot of North Hill and at the top of Link Common, the very popular Nag's Head pub was originally three small cottages, and has since been extended to give an interesting building with different floor levels and arched doorways. It is a free house and offers an excellent range of cask ales, including Pedigree, Shropshire Lad, and Funky Monkey (from Somerset). There is a wide choice of home-cooked food on the menu, and a selection of daily specials on the board. On our last visit we enjoyed traditional sausage and mash and sweet and sour pork. Lunch is available from 12 noon to 2 pm and evening food (6.30 pm to 8.30 pm) is served in the Nag's Tail function room. The small garden area is ideal for lunch on a sunny summer's day, and you might be lucky enough to see Morris dancers here. Telephone: 01684 574373.

- **HOW TO GET THERE:** Travelling south from Worcester on the A449, pass through Malvern Link and as the road climbs up to the top of the common and begins to bend left to Great Malvern, before reaching the traffic lights, fork left along Moorlands Road and go down about 50 yards to the Nag's Head.
- **PARKING:** There is parking at the pub and on adjacent roads.
- **LENGTH OF THE WALK:** 3½ miles. Map: OS Explorer 190 Malvern Hills and Bredon Hill (GR 776469).

THE WALK

1. From the Nag's Head walk up Bank Street passing the iron horses' heads on the wall by the door to number 19. At the crossroads, turn right along Zetland Road to climb up to the main road. The route turns left here, but a few yards to the right is the Morgan Inn, which contains interesting memorabilia of the Morgan car works.

Turn left for about 30 yards and then sharp right along North Malvern Road, towards the Tank Quarry. On the left is one of the few thatched houses in the area, and on the right is Holy Trinity church, dating from 1851 but enlarged in 1872. This is a fine building of local stone with the softer Cotswold limestone trim around windows and doors.

Just past Lodge Drive on the left are the old stocks and whipping post, with the stone pound behind, almost concealed by ivy. In front of these is Stocks Drinking Fountain, formerly a public drinking fountain, dating from 1895. The hill becomes clear to your left across the road, and on your right are a few shops and houses, as you approach the tower. Opposite the Tank Clock Tower is the old local stone building of the Morris School.

The walk goes up the steps behind the clock tower, but before starting on that path, it is worth going on a few yards to have a look at the second of the North Malvern quarries. A driveway leads into the Tank Quarry and the picnic place, but go up the steps to the right of the driveway for the view into the quarry, as well as

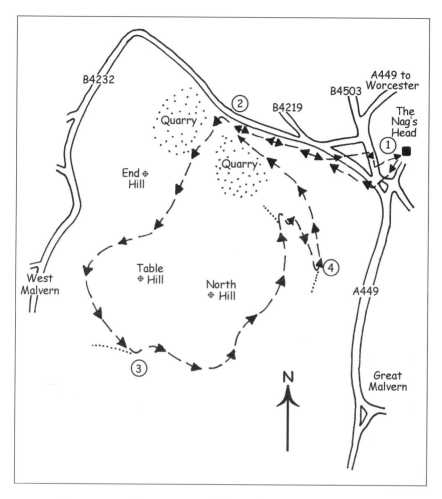

across the surrounding countryside to the east. Several boards give information about this quarry and its geology.

2. Now is the time to start the walk which will take you up beyond the top of the quarry. Brick steps lead up to a narrow footpath ascending steeply, and you soon have clear views into Tank Quarry to the right, and Scar Quarry to the left. The path splits; take the left fork to gain more height and quickly see good views to the left, down over the town and across the Severn Plain. Now climb steeply through the trees, passing occasional rocky outcrops. Ascend the narrow valley to emerge above the trees into an area of gorse and bracken with piles of lichen-encrusted rocks. Continue climbing

The Lady Howard de Walden Drive

straight up to the top of this valley to reach a broad and fairly level track, near two gnarled hawthorn trees and a simple wooden bench.

Here, turn right on the Lady Howard de Walden Drive. The broad path was created by the remarkable Lady de Walden who lived in St James, the large house at West Malvern, now part of a well-known girls' school. A great eccentric and a very wealthy widow, she provided money and labour to develop the circular route round North Hill in the 1890s, both for the sake of local people and also to allow herself to take a very scenic carriage drive.

The valley you climbed up is down to the right with End Hill beyond. As the track bends to the left, views open up over Herefordshire and into Wales. The route soon begins to descend and once round to the west side, fork left up a clear, stony track, before reaching the first house of West Malvern. As you climb up this track, the buildings of West Malvern soon come into sight, and the undulating landscape stretches away to the west. The higher ground consists of small hills, generally of limestone, and the dips are clay or sandstone, and each of these variations represents rocks of a different geological age – but all much younger than the rocks of the Malvern Hills. As you climb, good views southwards open up along the line of the Malvern ridge to the Iron Age fort on the Herefordshire Beacon and the Eastnor Obelisk.

3. The track levels off as you reach a col (a low pass), with views all round. Keep straight ahead here and descend slightly to a broad horizontal track. To the right you can see the Worcestershire Beacon; straight ahead is the Green or Happy Valley, leading down to St Ann's Well and the town centre. Turn left along the track, but soon bend right, with North Hill now up to the left. From the top of this hill (397m or 1,305 ft) there are wonderful all-round views, so if the weather is good and your legs are feeling strong, why not make a short detour here by forking left to go to the top?

If not, the onward route leads along this track, the de Walden Drive, climbing slightly, with views down into Happy Valley on the right. As the track bends left you can look down with an almost aerial view to Great Malvern with the Priory church looking like a small cathedral. Walk on round the top of a steep valley and after a further 250 yards look for the narrow but clear path going down to the right, just before a simple wooden bench. The path leads diagonally down the steep slope through bushes and small trees – look and listen for the wide variety of bird life here. At the first sharp elbow bend, across the plain you can spot the long avenue of trees lining the main driveway to Madresfield Court just beyond Madresfield church, and another straight line created by the railway line running between Malvern and Worcester. Follow this path as it zigzags down the steep slope, to reach another broad track, where you turn left.

4. Before turning left, just go a few yards right, to the large outcrop of Ivy Scar Rocks, slightly younger than the main mass of the Malverns, and intruded in a volcanic eruption. Wall pennywort with its bright green rounded leaves thrives on this outcrop.

After this detour follow the main track to descend to the car park by the Tank Clock Tower, where many trees have been planted to help hide the signs of quarrying. Walk out onto the road (point 2) and turn right to retrace your steps to the pub. On the way back down North Malvern Road, just before reaching the church, fork left down a narrow road with 'No Entry' for vehicles. Take care as there is no pavement for a few yards, but walk on down to the main road, cross at the pedestrian crossing, turn right and then left alongside The Vaults. This leads through to a small green surrounded by houses and over on the right side can be seen the Nag's Head and the starting point.

⑤ West Malvern
The Lamb

Though mainly on the west side of the hills, this walk takes us up to the Worcestershire Beacon, the highest point on the Malvern Hills (425m, 1,394 ft). From this summit you can look into at least eight counties on a clear day, and the toposcope will name many of the landmarks. We also visit Hay Slad, one of the largest springs on the hills, and pass through the old West Malvern quarries. These were purchased and closed by the Conservators in 1931, and we can admire and appreciate their excellent work in planting trees to screen the bare rock outcrops of the quarries, to create such an attractive landscape.

West Malvern straggles along the slopes on the hills and many of the houses here have steep drives and access routes, but are compensated by the spectacular views across Herefordshire into Wales. Morning views may be clearer but it is the afternoon and evening sunshine that the locals enjoy.

The Lamb is situated on the main road through West Malvern and its main bar and garden provide stunning views across the undulating Herefordshire countryside, where hills and valleys resemble a huge green corrugated sheet. It has been a pub for at least two generations, as recalled by local residents, and probably for much longer than 100 years. The building was formerly connected with farming and the main room, now a large bar, could have served as a barn, with its long, beamed ceiling. Downstairs in the cellar was a dairy, and perhaps a butcher's too, still retaining old hooks for hanging carcases. Food is served at lunchtime from 12 noon to 2 pm on Friday and Saturday and 12 noon to 3 pm on Sundays, and in the evening from 6 pm (7 pm on Saturdays) to 11 pm on Tuesday to Saturday. Everything is home cooked, and the claim to offer high quality cuisine is certainly justified. Baguettes, starters, main courses and delicious sweets will satisfy all tastes. I settled for the chicken supreme with an apricot sweet and sour sauce, accompanied by a choice of vegetables, which were cooked to perfection, and a pint of Adnam's bitter completed a very happy prelude to a walk on the hills behind the pub. Telephone: 01684 577847.

- **HOW TO GET THERE:** The Lamb will be found beside the B4232 which runs round the west side of the Malvern Hills between the Wyche Cutting and North Malvern.
- **PARKING:** There is parking at the rear of the pub.
- **LENGTH OF THE WALK:** 5 miles. Map: OS Explorer 190 Malvern Hills and Bredon Hill (GR 764470).

THE WALK

1. Up the steep road alongside the Lamb, walk between a few houses and when the narrow road ends take the surfaced path up to an old iron gate. If you think the views from here are good, you have much better still to come. Turn right along the path which begins to climb steadily near the backs of the houses. This is soon joined by a path from the left, and you continue to climb as the path becomes broader and quite stony. It moves further away from the houses, and views come and go and change rapidly as you pass through trees.

Ignore a path going to the left, but soon join a broad path coming down from the left, and the route levels off. A hedge is on your right with fields and views beyond, and the steep bracken and tree-covered hillside is to your left. Join a major stony track, and descend

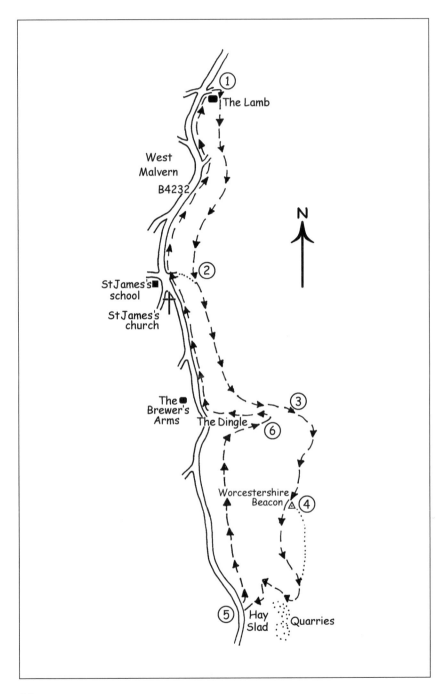

to pass a stone-built house on the right, and then reach a major junction of paths.

2. The sharp right turn would take you down into West Malvern near the church. Instead, go ahead, passing the Westminster Bank Spout on the left. Take the left hand track to go uphill, passing the Malvern Hills Conservators' 'No Wheeled Vehicles' notice. A sign pointing to the Beacon is concreted into the stonework surrounding the spout. Local houses formerly received their water supply from the storage chambers behind this spring, and to the west are underground tanks supplying St James's school with water. On hot days you might see dogs using this spring as a refreshing cooler.

You now begin to climb up a broad stony track, passing a small quarry (Westminster Quarry) on the left, with the valley of The Dingle down to the right.

3. At the top of this slope is a col, with a circular stone route guide, and the Beacon is to the right, along any one of several paths. With your back to the marker stone and looking up towards the Beacon, take the easiest option, which is the clear broad track heading slightly left. The track gradually swings round to the right as you ascend – and it remains dry in all but the wettest of weather. Views open up to the left over Worcestershire as you keep bearing to the right and soon the Beacon and the silhouette of the toposcope come into sight. Wind steadily up to the summit where the all-round views are quite stunning, and include the Wrekin, the Welsh Hills and the Cotswolds.

4. From the toposcope and the triangulation point, head westwards, going down across small paths for about 30 yards to reach the broad track where you turn left and head steadily downhill. The track is a mixture of grass and stones, and when views open up to the Worcestershire Plain to the left, look for the broad valley to your right. Just before you reach the tarmac track, fork right down a grassy path into this valley, and soon reach a broader path where you turn right and continue the descent. At a T-junction, with a seat just to the right, turn left and continue to go downhill. You are dropping into the old West Malvern quarries and straight ahead can be seen the top of the back wall of the largest of these quarries, just before the path turns right to descend a stone stepped path (which can be slippery if wet). At the bottom of this you reach the old quarry floor and turn right. You can glimpse the road through the fir trees on the left, and it is worth detouring down to the road near the

Looking west from Table Hill

layby. Cars are usually parked here whilst their owners fill water bottles from Hay Slad Spout, the largest of the Malvern Springs, which never dries up. Visitors come from many miles away to tap this source of free spring water.

5. Walk back up through the fir trees and turn left along the stony drive to reach a car parking area, then head diagonally right up and across the grassy patch to reach a horizontal path where you turn left. Walk alongside the stone wall surrounding lovely gardens, and continue along the top edge of another grassy patch to reach a major track. Turn right to go uphill through the trees. As you emerge from the trees, The Dingle slopes down to the left.

6. Go left into this valley and walk downhill on a grassy path passing Upper Dingle spring to reach a narrow surfaced road by the houses – the first on the right being Sugarloaf Cottage. Wonderful views across Herefordshire open up straight ahead as you descend. Pass a small quarry on the right and arrive at the road.

Turn right along the road, to reach a church and school. Walk through the churchyard, and carry on along the road, which in about ½ mile will take you back to the Lamb.

6 Stifford's Bridge
The Red Lion

Hills of limestone, often clothed in woodland and separated by deep green valleys, create the charming landscape to the west of the Malvern ridge. This short walk gives a taste of hills, woods, fields and a bubbling brook, and takes you from Stifford's Bridge into Cradley, a delightful village set in a farming area with many old black and white houses enhancing the landscape. The farmland is crossed by quiet country lanes, and does not attract large numbers of visitors, but is good walking territory with many footpaths and spectacular views.

In Cradley itself is the church of St James, largely restored in 1868-70, its nave being the work of Sir George Gilbert Scott. The register goes back to 1560, but a church has been here for much longer; the upper part of the tower as well as parts of the stalls date from the 15th century and the timber-framed lychgate is medieval. Fine views over the wooded hills can be seen from the top of the tower. Further along the lane is the black and white Church Cottage, whilst on the left is the village hall, a 15th century timber-framed building which has served as a boys' school in the past.

The Red Lion at Stifford's Bridge is a free house offering a good range of beers, with Hobsons ever popular, also Stowford cider and a wide selection of wine. The black and white building is an old coaching inn and has been enlarged. There are two dining areas and two lounges, with modern fittings but an old-style cosy feel to the layout. Outside, the children's playground and attractive small garden with patio and fishpond are away from the main road. The food is outstanding, whether for large or small gatherings or large or small appetites. Everything is home cooked and the menu board changes daily. From sandwiches to full scale meals there is ample choice and the home-made pies are particularly popular. There is a variety of vegetarian food – up to eight different dishes – and a pensioners' board offering special two-course lunches. The opening times are 12 noon to 3 pm and 6 pm to 11 pm, with food from 12 noon to 2 pm and 6.30 pm to 9.30 pm (no food is served on Sunday evenings). Telephone: 01886 880318.

- **HOW TO GET THERE:** Stifford's Bridge is on the A4103 Worcester–Hereford road, to the west of Leigh Sinton and Storridge.
- **PARKING:** The Red Lion has a large parking area.
- **LENGTH OF THE WALK:** 2½ miles. Map: OS Explorer 190 Malvern Hills and Bredon Hill (GR 734481).

THE WALK

1. Turn left from the pub and walk along the verge for about 80 yards. Just before the two cottages (white and pink), take the narrow path through trees alongside the edge of the garden. The path leads through to a stile and beyond this we follow the left margin of the field to a stile in the corner and continue on the left margin of an apple orchard. Reach a drive then go up some steps, over a stile and along the side of a small paddock. Wold Farm, to the left, is noted for its cider and perry. Slope down to a stile – then a drive and another stile – with a delightful black and white house on the left. Ten yards beyond the second stile, turn left over another stile to go through the hedge, into a small field, and follow the path leading to a gated footbridge over Cradley Brook.

2. The path heads diagonally left across the field to a stile and on to a driveway. Cross straight over to another stile and follow the line

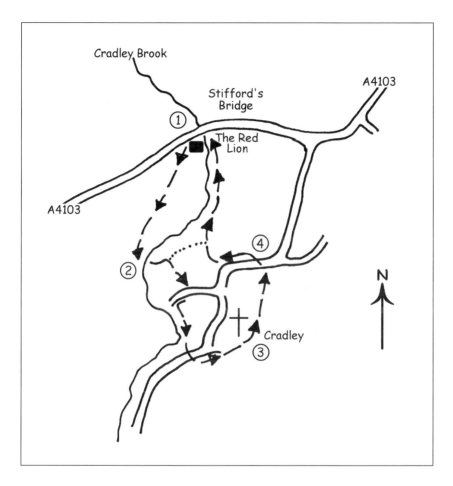

of trees forming a hedge to the right. Ahead, the squat tower of Cradley church comes into sight, with the wooded Lambridge Hill beyond. Descend slightly to the edge of the field and a stile. Go over this and turn right along the narrow road, as far as Brook Cottage - on the right. Turn left here, over a stile and along the left margin of a grassy field. The brook is down to the right. At the next stile go into a small wood, and pass a notice saying you are entering a 'Private Garden' - but it is a right-of-way. A variety of firs clothe the slope down to the right; pass between hedges and gardens to reach a narrow road. Turn left here, passing the Cradley Village School as you climb steadily up to the war memorial and a small green - with the church beyond.

3. Visit the splendid church, with a well-kept churchyard. Near the porch stands a sundial on a weathered stone plinth, with its notice mentioning that it was restored for the Jubilee of Queen Victoria, 21st June 1887. From the lychgate proceed along Rectory Lane, and on the right of this stony track is the delightful Church Cottage. On your left is the old village hall. No-one could possibly walk past without pausing in admiration. Beyond the hall, when the lane ends go over the stile and turn left along the field margin. There are good views all around, with wooded hills and sheltered green valleys dotted with black and white houses. Traditionally the lush fields are home to sheep and cattle, but nowadays contain many horses too. Follow the left margin of the field and descend to the stile, cross the stream and over another stile, to continue along the left margin of the next field. The exit from this field is over an unusual stile fixed to the metal gate.

4. At the road turn left, to pass a bus stop on the left (the Worcester–Ledbury service passes here from Monday to Saturday, and there is a Friday only service between Cradley and Malvern) and a small modern development of housing on the right, behind the old black and white Buryfield Cottage. Follow the road as it descends between older housing, including the thatched Barratts Cottage. As the road bends left, go right at the footpath sign which points along a driveway past a white gate. Follow this stony drive and when it splits fork right towards Windrush and a large wooden gate with a stile alongside. Go over the stile and straight ahead, with the winding stream down to your left lined with leafy willow trees. Go through the kissing gate at the end of this field and veer slightly left to come closer to the stream where Himalayan balsam is thriving – and very colourful. By now, somewhere on this walk you will probably have seen and heard two of my favourite Malvern birds, buzzard and raven. Favourites because they are large and easily seen as they float around overhead and they have the decency to call to make sure you are aware of their existence. Pass through another small kissing gate, by a larger gate, and keep straight ahead to the iron kissing gate and the main road. The Red Lion is to your left.

⑦ Mathon
The Cliffe Arms

Undulations and the green landscape are the essence of this circuit from the Cliffe Arms, with the Welsh Hills providing a panoramic view to the west. We cross the tiny Cradley Brook, follow paths across fields and through woods, with the Malvern ridge just 2 miles to the east. The village of Mathon and the isolated houses and farms all merge into this beautiful rural area. It has been claimed there is no finer scenery in England, which is quite appropriate to Mathon, the name being derived from the Old English word for treasure or gift.

Mathon village spreads along the narrow country lanes, from the church in the west to the village hall in the east, and is surrounded by farmland. Hops were formerly important but now the fields are mainly used for grazing. Local quarries yielded sand and gravel but the diggings have now ceased, leaving only small lakes as a reminder of the activity. The church of St John the Baptist dates from the 11th century and near the door is a large stone where locals paid their tithe money and could hire their labourers. Next door to the church is the former village school, now a private house.

The Cliffe Arms is just along the road from the church, and has been a pub for several hundred years. Formerly two or three small cottages, its partial flagstone floor is very ancient as are the low beams – which need constant care if you are tall. The walls are decorated with old maps and photographs. This olde worlde free house serves Adnams bitter as well as Fuller's London Pride, and boasts a comprehensive wine list. All food is home cooked and there are daily changes to the menu, which ranges from baguettes to large steaks and pasta. The public bar, the restaurant in the old barn at the rear and the spacious garden provide ample room for eating. Food is served Wednesday to Sunday lunchtime between 11 am and 2.30 pm and on Tuesday to Sunday evenings from 6.30 pm to 11 pm.

- **HOW TO GET THERE:** Take the B4232 to West Malvern, and near the church and St James's School follow the narrow road signed westwards to Mathon.
- **PARKING:** There is plenty of car parking at the front and side of the pub.
- **LENGTH OF THE WALK:** $4\frac{1}{2}$ miles. Map: OS Explorer 190 Malvern Hills and Bredon Hill (GR 736458).

THE WALK

1. Turn right from the Cliffe Arms and after about 40 yards go right over a stile along a narrow path between gardens. Cross the footbridge over Cradley Brook, to reach a track, and fork slightly right. Follow this stony track across fields, as it bends right to begin a gentle climb. Look back to enjoy good views to Mathon church tower. When the drive bends left to the gate of a house called Overley, go right over a stile and across a small field to another stile, and on to a track.

Turn left here, by the limestone quarry. Sharp-eyed walkers may see fossils in these rocks – small shelly animals called brachiopods are quite common. They must have been very numerous in the warm seas where these rocks were formed in the Silurian period about 420 million years ago.

Walk along the track, passing above the house to your left, and keep ahead through the next field.

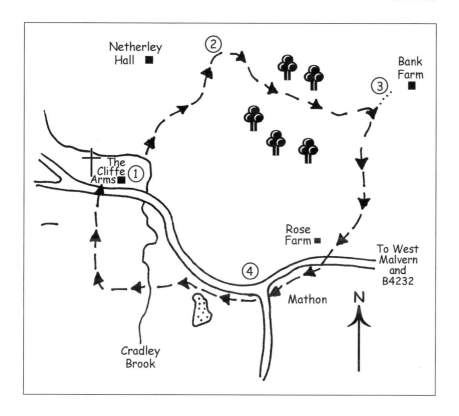

2. Before you get to Netherley Hall, those magnificent buildings to the left, the path divides and you fork right. Keep ahead until reaching the track coming from Netherley, where you turn right, to follow the field margin and a small gully. As you approach the corner of the woods, before reaching the gate ahead (with a 'Private' notice), move to the right and begin the steep climb up Cockshot Hill, along the top margin of the field – with wonderful views across the countryside to the west. Can you spot Cradley church with the black and white village hall next door to it (see Walk 6)?

Go over the stile into the woods, and follow the clear path as it leads through to a broad track, where you turn left. The track divides and you keep straight ahead, and walk alongside the fence with an open field sloping down to the right. More views open up here, including the mast on the hill near Much Marcle. Straight ahead on the walk can be seen the main Malvern ridge. Just follow the track to a gathering of gates. Walk straight ahead and onto a stony driveway, soon to reach the next gateway, beyond which the buildings of Bank Farm are to the left.

3. After a further 20 yards turn right, at the first gate, to go down the delightful green valley to a stile by a gate. Keep ahead through the next two fields and come to a stony track on the edge of a small wood. Beyond this go through a gate and another field to reach a stile and walk down to the very impressive barn conversions (a Grade II listed barn). Turn left down the drive to reach the narrow road, where you turn right. An orchard is on the right and the buildings of Rose Farm can be seen adjacent to the modernised barns.

4. Fork right at the road junction, passing a couple of houses and Mathon Village Hall. Shortly beyond here as the road bends right, keep straight ahead along the track signed to Warner's Farm; on your left is a pool – a former gravel working. Pass to the right of a house and a Caravan Club site, to reach a stile, and continue along the left side of the field to a stiled footbridge over Cradley Brook. From the bridge turn right to head across a narrow field to a stile and go on along the left margin of the next field, climbing slightly. There are wonderful views again – and you can work out where you have been walking for the last hour or so.

At the end of the field go over a stile to a crossing point of paths. Turn right and follow this narrow footpath between hedges. It soon widens to a track and leads to a gate, the road and the church. Turn right, passing the old school on the left, and walk back to the pub.

8 **Great Malvern**
The Mount Pleasant Hotel

If you want a short walk (1 hour or so) repaid by inspirational views over Malvern and beyond, this is the route for you. It not only gives a wonderful reward for a brief, but very steep climb, it also explores part of this Victorian town.

The Mount Pleasant is an elegant early Georgian building dating from 1730 and subsequently used as a hotel for the Water Cure, which contributed so much to the growth of Malvern. A new wing was added in 1850, attached to what is now Lloyds bank, and there has been much recent renovation, within the old framework. One of the fascinating relics of the past is the original bowl from St Ann's Well, which is set just outside the door leading from the car park into Reception. The eminent local matriarch Lady Emily Foley presented a new bowl to St Ann's, and this will be seen on the walk.

The terraced garden extends up the slope as far as the Orangery – no longer part of the hotel. The Mount Pleasant offers en-suite accommodation, as well as menus in the Coffee Shop, Lounge Bar and Restaurant. It is a free house serving a variety of beers, but equally tempting may be the range of wines, with over 30 available by the glass, including three local labels. Food is served from 10.30 am until 10.30 pm, and whether you want a jacket potato, soup of the day or the full meal, the choice is all there. Sunday lunch is one of many specialities. Local dishes such as Herefordshire beef, cheeses and ice creams are featured. Children are always welcome – and so are dogs. Telephone: 01684 561837.

- **HOW TO GET THERE:** The Mount Pleasant is located on the fairly level Belle Vue Terrace, which is on the main A449 Worcester-Ledbury road, and at the top of the steeply sloping main street in Great Malvern.
- **PARKING:** In the Mount Pleasant car park or in one of the several fee paying car parks in the town.
- **LENGTH OF THE WALK:** Just over a mile, but with possible detours you may take more than an hour. Stop and admire the views, frequently! Map: OS Explorer 190 Malvern Hills and Bredon Hill (GR 775459). A series of three more detailed maps of the hills can be bought at the Tourist Information Centre, on a scale of 1:10,000.

THE WALK

1. Turn left from the pub and walk along the main road, Belle Vue Terrace. In the well-kept gardens across the road is a lifesize statue of Sir Edward Elgar and the Malvhina spring – two modern additions to this Victorian town. Local sculptor Rose Garrard designed the spout, which takes its name from a legendary Gaelic princess. The water is collected from three springs higher up the hillside.

Pass a few shops which were part of the original Belle Vue Hotel, to reach Robson Ward, Designer Furniture, and in their courtyard is a spring which was the first source of bottled water in Malvern. Next you reach the Unicorn, an ancient pub formerly on the stagecoach route to Worcester. You turn left here, up St Ann's Road, following the sign to Worcestershire Beacon, Sugar Loaf, Table and North Hills via Happy Valley.

A very steep climb takes you past the Red Lion pub on the right, and soon St Ann's Road turns left. But, no relief yet, as you keep straight ahead. Look out for the old gas lamp standards, and after about 50 yards on the right there are the old wooden sheds which

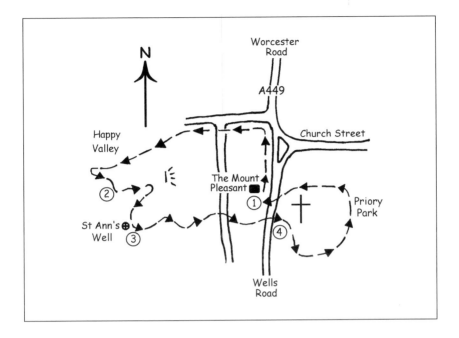

were donkey houses. In Victorian times, ladies, and sometimes gentlemen, did not consider walking up the hills, and instead were carried on donkeys – providing a lucrative source of income for the donkey owners.

Just past the last house on the left notice a stream flowing in the channel on your left – it emerges from a spring higher up Happy Valley. Soon reach the end of the narrow surfaced road, where a path goes right here to Ivy Scar Rocks, and a track keeps straight ahead up Happy Valley.

2. Turn sharp left along the broad stony track signed to St Ann's Well and the Beacon. A few more minutes of climbing and you emerge from the trees to find wonderful panoramic views across the Severn Plain to the Cotswolds, with Malvern down at your feet. St Ann's Well and your onward route are to the right and downhill. But first, walk across the grass and sit on the seat to admire the bird's eye view over the heart of the town with the Priory church particularly prominent.

The building at St Ann's Well dates from 1815, and the octagonal extension is from 1843. Inside the building is the spring, with plaque and information board. The spout and basin of Sicilian marble were the gift of Lady Foley in 1892. A memorial plaque on the outside wall remembers George Pullen, 'Blind George', who played the harmonium (now in the museum) here for about 50 years. For modern visitors there is now a café providing excellent refreshments.

3. From the well walk down the steep and winding road, noting the eco-friendly restored toilet building to the right, with a grass covered roof – the work of the Malvern Hills Conservators. More of the famous Malvern old-fashioned gas lamp standards line this road, and as we descend new views open up on every bend. Just before reaching the fairly level St Ann's Road at a T-junction the Mount Pleasant and its gardens can be seen. Turn right at the road, and as it divides after 20 yards fork left on the drive towards Half Way and Bello Sguardo (built in the 19th century on the site of a former hermitage), and then fork left to descend the steps. These lead down into Rose Bank Gardens, and level with the last step, through a gap in the wall, we can see the Orangery. The information board tells us that these gardens were restored by Malvern Hills District Council in 1996, opened by Sir Roy Strong on 21st September. The gardens had originally been given by C.W. Dyson Perrins of the Lea and Perrins factory, a benefactor to Malvern in several other ways.

We are now back to the starting point but if you have a few more minutes cross over the road towards the Abbey Hotel, which is just through the old archway, the former gateway of the Priory. Given to the Malvern Museum Society by the De Vere Hotels who formerly owned the Abbey Hotel, it now houses the museum. Exhibitions of Malvern's history and local geology are amongst the interesting displays within.

4. If you walk on past the hotel and turn left, the Malvern Theatres as well as Priory Park are only a few yards ahead. To return to the Mount Pleasant, turn left up the alleyway between stone walls, opposite the main entrance to the theatre. This takes you round the Priory church passing the east wall with its stone plaque memorial to local people killed in World War I. The interior is well worth visiting – if you have an hour or so to spare, but otherwise just walk uphill through the churchyard, with its varied assortment of trees, to return to Belle Vue.

⑨ Barnard's Green
The Bluebell

Our walk takes in delightful reminders of Victorian Malvern, as we stroll past Great Malvern station and the homes of Doctors Gully and Wilson, key personalities in the Malvern Water Cure, before stretching our legs for a brisk walk across the Malvern commons. The Bluebell is at the western end of the tree-lined Guarlford Road as it approaches Barnard's Green, with a backcloth of the hills.

Barnard's Green now merges with Malvern as it stretches from the plain to the lower slopes of the hills. With its own shopping area, the Green is a vibrant centre, bustling with shoppers and motorists. A small flower-covered green is at its heart, and a pleasant pool is situated on the eastern fringe near the Bluebell.

A big pub, with a big menu, the Bluebell is always busy, and serves food throughout the day, from 12 noon to 9 pm (9.30 pm at weekends) – very useful for walkers who like to eat at the end of their exertions, whether it is 5 pm or 8 pm. The main bar area is part of an ancient building with old beams, but modern beams are exposed in the more recent extensions. The pub is part of the Wolverhampton and Dudley Breweries and a variety of beers and cider are on offer together with an extensive wine list. The menu is wide ranging, with regular daily additions on the blackboard. Main meals, light bites and sandwiches are available as well as vegetarian dishes. Opening hours for drinks are 11 am to 11 pm on Monday to Saturday and 12 noon to 10.30 pm on Sunday. Telephone 01684 575031.

- **HOW TO GET THERE:** The Bluebell is on Guarlford Road, the B4211 on the east side of Great Malvern, close to its junction with the B4208.
- **PARKING:** The inn has a large car park.
- **LENGTH OF THE WALK:** 5 miles. Map: OS Explorer 190 Malvern Hills and Bredon Hill (GR 793454).

THE WALK

1. Leave the pub and turn left to walk alongside the road on the margin of the grass. Pass alongside the Hastings Pool and cross to the pavement with a stone wall and the delightful gardens of Barnards Green House on the left. The house was the home of Sir Charles Hastings, founder of the British Medical Association, and the lovingly maintained gardens are open on Thursday afternoons in the summer. Walk on between the shops of Barnard's Green to the large kidney-shaped island. Take the second exit, Avenue Road, signed to Christ Church and Malvern Girls' College. This tree-lined road with more trees in large gardens still benefits from the original building plan. Housing plots had to be large, and trees had to be planted according to the instructions of Lady Emily Foley. Lady Foley was widowed in 1846 and she managed her husband's estates, including much of Malvern, in a firm and decisive fashion, until the end of the century.

Pass Christ Church, on the right, and then the wonderful old Imperial Hotel, now the main building of the Girls' College. Notice the stone carvings on the pillars. If you cross over to the right side of the road at the railway bridge, down below you is a covered walkway, known as 'the worm', no longer in use but designed to allow Victorian visitors to walk from the station into the hotel without exposure to the weather. The hotel was built in 1861–62 by E.W. Elmslie, who also built the station.

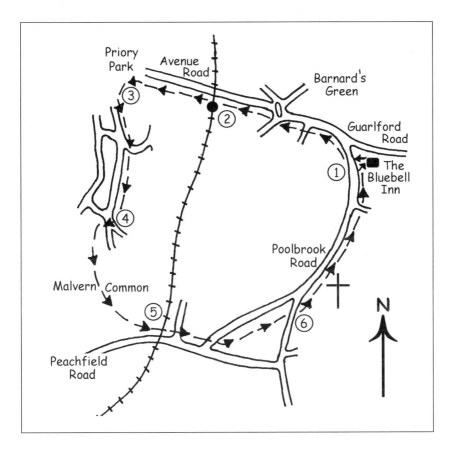

2. It is worth a detour to the station to look at the decorated pillars and other Victorian features. There is a tearoom that bears Lady Foley's name – useful if you need refreshment. In her later years she retained a waiting room on the platform for her own private use until the train arrived. She lived at Stoke Edith in Herefordshire but would not travel through the tunnel beneath the hills from Colwall station so came to Malvern by carriage.

The walk continues up Avenue Road, and as you cross over Priory Road, note the large monkey puzzle tree on the corner. Before reaching the main road, turn left into the car parking area for the Malvern Hills District Council Offices. Walk on past the large building on your left, noting the Civic Society plaque mentioning that this is 'The Site of Priory House, the residence and consulting rooms of Dr. James Manby Gully 1847–1872'.

The fluted pillar box, passed en route

3. Walk into the park, passing the Splash Fitness Centre on the left, cross the footbridge over Swan Pool, pass the bandstand and walk on towards the steps leading into the theatre. Turn left at the foot of the steps to walk towards the exit from the park, with the Priory church coming into view from behind the theatre. This park contains a variety of trees including the magnolia and the handkerchief tree – well worth a wander if you find trees of interest.

Leave the park and emerge onto the road. Up to the right is a large green building, Park View, now a block of flats, but built in 1845 for Doctor James Wilson's hydropathic treatment. On the left is a bowling green and as you approach the end of this road, Orchard Road, notice the rare fluted pillar box on the right side. Cross to College Road, with St Edmunds on the left, formerly a Catholic church but now part of Malvern College, founded in 1862.

Walk on, passing boys' boarding houses and the main college buildings on the left.

Once past the main entrance to the college, the road bends to the right, but you turn left here.

4. After about 20 yards, by the post box in the wall, cross over and head up the narrow path, known locally as The Chimney. At the top of this path turn left along the stony track, passing a thatched house on the left, to emerge on the edge of the common. A selection of trees and shrubs can be seen over this wall, with a fine display of bluebells in May. At the end of the wall, and just before reaching a small pond, fed by a spring from the hills, turn left to go down the common. Once heading down the Wells Common, aim for the far right corner.

5. At the bottom of the common join the road to cross over the railway bridge, and on your right can be seen a white house with a small building beyond in its gardens. This was formerly the waiting room for Malvern Wells station which no longer exists.

Follow the pavement and keep ahead, passing another of the fluted Victorian pillar boxes (designed by Smith and Hawke about 1857 – only five remain in England and three of them are in Malvern). Cross two roads turning left and only then move away from the road as you reach the open space of Poolbrook Common – with Bredon Hill straight ahead, about 10 miles to the east. Head slightly left across the middle of this common towards a white house and a stone church. Keep to the right of the damp patch in the lowest part, shown clearly by the different water-loving grasses, to pass a flat patch also used as a football pitch. No sign of David Beckham but some very enthusiastic players turn out here at the weekends.

6. Cross over the road at the bottom of the common and continue to bear slightly left, to walk along to the church of St Andrew, built of local granite. The common narrows as you pass the Three Horseshoes, with the road to your left and good views to the hills beyond. Follow the line of the road, to retrace your steps to the Bluebell.

⑩ Malvern Wells
The Railway Inn

Moving away from the hills, we follow the edge of one of Malvern's extensive commons, before strolling alongside the picturesque golf course and making a circuit around the Three Counties Showground, famous for its annual agricultural show. Our return route crosses fields and then follows an old railway line before climbing back up towards the hills and the Railway Inn. There is a chance to extend the walk into the lovely Langdale Wood - an extra 2 miles if you wish.

The growth of Malvern really began at Malvern Wells - though subsequent growth was mainly in Great Malvern. Visitors flocked here, initially to the ancient Holy Well as early as the mid 18th century. One of the oldest buildings nearby is the Ruby, just along the road from the Railway Inn. The house was named after Admiral Benbow's last ship, and was the home for a time of Hugh Boyd, the blind classics scholar, a great friend of Elizabeth Barrett. She regularly walked here from her home near Wellington Heath. Also just along the road from the Railway is Craeglea (an anagram of the initial letter of Edward, Alice and Carice and the surname), Elgar's home for five years from 1899.

The Railway Inn is located alongside the A449 Malvern–Ledbury road – enjoying views across the Wells Common. The pub was owned by the Great Western Railway in the 19th century, and was popular with local quarrymen as well as the diggers cutting the rail tunnel through to Colwall (opened in 1861). Lengths of old railway line can be seen in the fence between the car park and the main road. The bar and restaurant area are bright and spacious and a small patio and terrace are popular in sunny weather. Part of the Wolverhampton and Dudley Breweries, the pub offers a good choice of beers including Banks's and Marston's Pedigree real ales, and as many as seven varieties of wine available by the glass. All food is freshly cooked and there is a wide menu, especially noted being the traditional Sunday lunch – for which booking is advisable. Local vegetables are offered whenever possible and several vegetarian dishes are served. Opening hours for food are 12 noon to 2.30 pm and 6.30 pm to 9.30 pm. Telephone: 01684 572168.

- **HOW TO GET THERE:** The Railway Inn is on the west side of the A449 at the northern edge of Malvern Wells, overlooking the Wells Common.
- **PARKING:** Parking is available at the pub and along the roadside.
- **LENGTH OF THE WALK:** 5 miles, with an extra 2 miles if the circuit round Langdale Wood is added. Map: OS Explorer 190 Malvern Hills and Bredon Hill (GR 772439).

THE WALK

1. Cross the road and walk down the edge of the common, and before reaching the bottom, turn right along Peachfield Close into the housing development called Fruitlands. Go over the cattle grid which reveals something of the animal life to be seen on the common. Walk along the pavement, following the road as it winds slightly, passing Mulberry Drive and Walnut Drive which go left down to the railway line. Once beyond Cherry Tree Drive look for the track and bridleway going left to pass beneath the railway line and out onto the picturesque golf course.

Follow the marker posts to the right of the ponds and along the path, to reach a major path where the bridleway goes left.

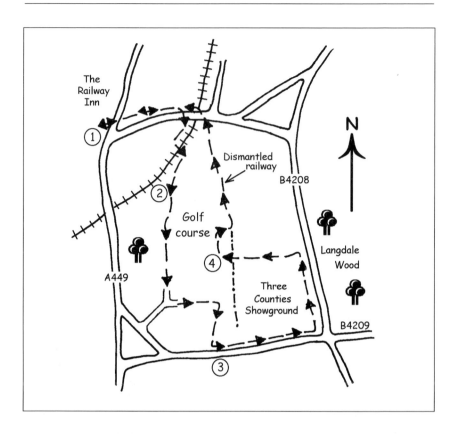

2. Turn right here. Pass to the right of the new club house and continue along the road leading away from the course. After a few houses on the right, and then more on the left, cross over a stream.

As the road bends right, with paths to left and right, go left along a track, through to a gate and stile. Walk on along the left margin of the field, to a stile and footbridge, then onto the track. Turn right, to pass between the buildings of Coton Cottage Farm. The modernised buildings are of brick and others are local stone, some used as stables.

3. At the road turn left, to pass a few cottages on the left and Brickbarns Farm on the right. Keep going along the pavement with the Three Counties Showground site on the left.

At the crossroads turn left on the B4208 towards Great Malvern, to pass several gates going left into the showground, and on the right is an area of woodland. At the last gate, the Yellow, there is a small car park area and on the opposite side of the road is the entrance to Langdale Wood - a delightful walk and full of interest for bird lovers. The circuit round these woods is clearly signed with marker posts and will add nearly 2 miles to the walk, but might enable you to hear a nightingale.

The return to the starting point is about 2 miles from here. Follow the footpath sign and go through the large metal gate on the left of the road, just beyond the small car park. Stay close to the hedge on the left, heading towards the hills. At the end of the field go through a gate, and straight ahead across another smaller field, and then a third field, which is an old orchard leading up slightly to a gate and onto the old railway embankment.

4. Follow the track to the other side of the old embankment, where you turn sharp right alongside a narrow field on the right. At the end of this turn right beneath the railway bridge, and where the drive goes right, to Warren Farm, go left over a stile, to walk along the left margin of the field. This leads to a stile and over a stream. Continue along the next field as it climbs slightly, where the railway embankment has become a cutting. In the corner of the field go through an iron gate and straight across the track, over the stile and up steps onto the line of the old railway. This will lead you between a field on the right and the golf course on the left, in its wonderful setting. Reach the road, where you turn left, to walk over the railway bridge and follow the edge of the common alongside this road, climbing steadily back up to the pub at the top of the common. Enjoy the last of many wonderful views to the hills as you walk this final stretch.

⑪ Wyche
The Wyche Inn

Starting from the highest pub on the ridge we can enjoy the views without any strenuous walking, as we follow a gentle path to St Ann's Well. Next we climb up higher through trees to reach the open grassy hilltop for yet more views, before descending past the Gold Mine – where an unsuccessful search for gold was made in the 18th century.

The Wyche Cutting, a dramatic gash in the hills, is the route of a pre-Roman saltway from Droitwich to Herefordshire. The settlement of The Wyche is perched on both sides of the hills close to the cutting – and is quite Alpine in character with houses clinging to the steep slope.

Painted white and clearly visible from out on the plain, the lights of the Wyche Inn stand out brightly at night, and can be seen from as far away as Upton. The old stone building dates from the 17th century and was originally a row of cottages. The two long and spacious bars are on two levels, the lower one with pool and darts as well as tables. A small conservatory and patio area are used if the weather is good. But, wherever you sit, the views across the plain are stunning. The beers are good too, with the line-up including three real ales, a favourite being the local brew Hobsons from Cleobury Mortimer. You might like to try the international flavour of San Miguel lager – and think of sunny Spain. The large wine list includes the delightfully named Old Git. Food is served daily from 12 noon to 9 pm, with a particular bargain being the roast lunch on Sunday (booking is advisable). A wide choice is available from the regular menu as well as the board which has frequently-changing specials. The range will satisfy all appetites – sandwiches or snacks as well as full meals, with several home-made specialities such as lasagne and Giant Yorkshire Pudding filled with chicken curry, also vegetarian dishes. It has been rumoured that Elgar visited the Wyche Inn but it is certain that the more modern musician Nigel Kennedy has been here. If you fancy another day in the hills tomorrow, accommodation is available, in en-suite rooms. Telephone: 01684 575396.

- **HOW TO GET THERE:** The Wyche Inn is easily found near the top of the slope up from Malvern on the B4218 towards Colwall.
- **PARKING:** Park in the small car park or along the roadside.
- **LENGTH OF THE WALK:** 4 miles. Map: OS Explorer 190 Malvern Hills and Bredon Hill (GR 770438).

THE WALK

1. From the pub door cross over the road to enjoy the wonderful view across the Severn Plain to the Cotswolds – one of the finest views in England. In the afternoon sun with the light shining from the west, Upton church spire glows in the sunshine, and the Cotswolds look incredibly close. Turn left to walk downhill and soon pass the Upper Wyche Quarry on the left, but keep going as far as Earnslaw Quarry. Cross over (with care) and turn to the right corner of this quarry car park. Follow the path with a concrete sign placed in the wall, pointing to Earnslaw and The Beacon. The broad path soon divides; take the right fork.

As the path leaves the trees for an open grassy patch, your onward route is down to the right, but first, go left for a few yards and up the steps to look down into Earnslaw Quarry. The lake is cold and dangerous, though picturesque and containing fish, stocked by the Malvern Hills Conservators. As you descend along the broad path,

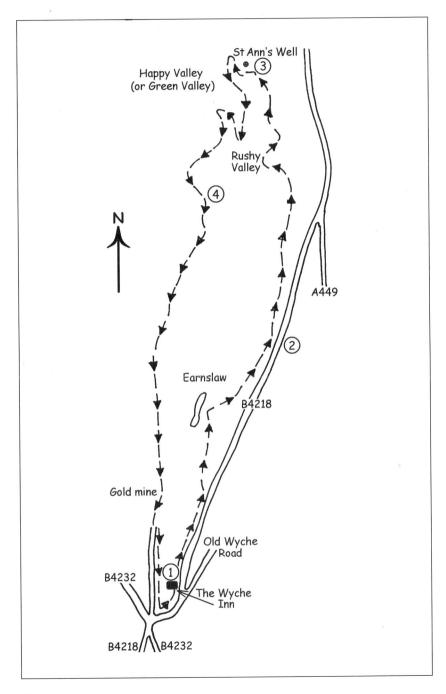

views open up to Malvern, with the spire of Christ Church and the imposing building of the old Imperial Hotel, now part of Malvern Girls' College.

2. Descend nearly to the road, but veer left away from it, to pass another concrete sign in the wall (pointing back to The Wyche) and the memorial seat to Con and Lena, then ascend slightly but continue along a fairly level route through trees. This firm gravel and stone path undulates and winds but will lead to St Ann's Well. On the way you pass the steep Rushy Valley, with piles of rocks to the left and right of the path. Up to the left, near the top of this valley is the Dripping Well, the highest spring on the hills, which continues to flow, or trickle, even in prolonged dry spells in summer. At St Ann's Well, a restorative cup of tea may be available, as well as toilets. This famous well has a plaque and information board inside the building above the spring, and outside the door is a small plaque memorial to 'Blind George', George Pullen, who used to walk here each day to play his harmonium. The spring flows into the Dolphin spout and bowl, which together with the marble tablet was provided by Lady Emily Foley in 1892. The verse was written by Rev W. Blake Atkinson – 'Drink of this crystal fountain'.

3. The onward route is to the left of the building, passing behind the well and climbing steadily to where the track divides. Fork left here and after a few metres fork left again, and walk uphill through the trees – soon to emerge into a grassy area with St Ann's down to the left.

Coming above the trees there may be a change in the climate, and certainly in winter an extra layer is required as you move out towards the open hilltop. Even in summer it is surprising how different conditions are here, as compared with down in the town.

Follow this grassy track as it climbs to reveal the views out left over Malvern and the Severn Plain. By a small simple bench on the left, a narrow path goes straight ahead towards the Dripping Well and Rushy Valley but your broad path bends sharp right and continues to climb. To your right look across to North Hill beyond the deep valley (Happy Valley). When two or three grassy paths can be seen ahead, your route bends sharp left, still on a broad grassy track, and gradually bends right to circle the upper part of Rushy Valley. As you head on towards the Worcestershire Beacon, looking up to the right it is possible to see the toposcope silhouetted on the summit. Still climbing slightly, with bracken on both sides, you reach

Refreshments can be found at St Ann's Well

an area of bilberry and at another bench, where the main track bends sharp right, the footpath goes straight ahead.

4. The footpath from the bench is fairly level and cuts across to join the surfaced track linking the summit with The Wyche. Once on this track the views open up across to the Herefordshire side of the hills, to reveal a different landscape from the Worcestershire side. The geology of the western side has contributed to the alternation of hills and vales in Herefordshire. The hills are mostly limestone and the vales are clays or shales, and all these rocks, though old (more than 400 million years), are much younger than the Malvern Hills.

As you descend steadily, the nucleated settlement of Colwall is down to the right, and along the line of the hills you will see the silhouette of the Herefordshire Beacon with the Eastnor Obelisk just to the right. On a clear day the clump of trees on the summit of May Hill will be visible in the distance. Pass the stone marker named 'The Gold Mine', and reach the end of the car parking area. At the road, turn left to walk round to the Wyche Inn and the starting point.

⑫ Upper Colwall
The Chase Inn

From the secluded and sheltered wooded slopes we climb up to the different world of the open and often windswept hilltop to enjoy wide views across the surrounding lowlands of Herefordshire and Worcestershire. The walk can be comfortably completed in two hours – even allowing time to have a breather.

Chase Road is merely a ribbon of houses forming part of Upper Colwall – and facing the evening sun. The Chase Inn is one of a row of houses which has been extended several times in the past. Formerly a bakery as well as a private house, it was granted inn status in 1869, and originally brewed its own beer. Hanging baskets decorate the front, but they are merely a small taster of what can be seen in the garden at the rear. Immaculate, colourful for most of the year and with views across to the west, this is a haven of peace and tranquillity. The food is home cooked and delicious, with daily changes to the menu. On our last visit we chose the avocado and prawn salad with new potatoes, and the home-baked ham with salad and fries – both delicious. A good variety of real ales, from Donnington (their SBA is highly recommended), Hobsons and Wye Valley, are available as well as the local Stowford cider from Much Marcle. The opening times are 12 noon to 2.30 pm and 6 pm to 11 pm Monday to Saturday, and 12 noon to 2 pm and 7 pm to 10.30 pm on Sunday. Food is served lunchtime only from 12 noon to 2.30 pm but not on Sunday or Tuesday lunchtime. Telephone: 01684 540276.

- **HOW TO GET THERE:** Take the B4218 from Malvern to Colwall, and shortly beyond the Wyche Cutting fork left along Chase Road, where the major road going downhill to Colwall has a very sharp right bend. The Chase Inn is on the right.
- **PARKING:** Parking is available on the roadside near the inn or in the small quarry opposite.
- **LENGTH OF THE WALK:** 3 miles. Map: OS Explorer 190 Malvern Hills and Bredon Hill (GR 766430).

THE WALK

1. Leave the pub and turn right to walk along the road for 500 yards, with houses on the right and the wooded slope on the left. As the road begins to climb and bend to the right, look for the path on the left, where you take a sharp turn along the broad way heading up through the trees. Reach the higher road and cross to a path a few yards to the left. Go up this narrow and steep path heading diagonally left for about 20 yards to reach a clear horizontal path where you turn right. Follow this path, parallel to the road which is a few yards down to the right, and gradually views begin to open up to the right – through the trees.

2. As you come adjacent to the road, with the Kettle Sings café just visible across to the right, turn sharp left just before reaching Gardiner's Quarry. Named after the family who worked the quarry, it is now used as a parking area.

When you reach another broad track, turn left. Notice the coniferous woodland called Thirds Land on the left – the only plantation on the Malverns ridge. Views open up across to the right over Worcestershire. The track splits into three and you take the middle route to climb the short steep slope up to the next knob along the ridge top. This small peak, at a height of 327m (1,073 ft)

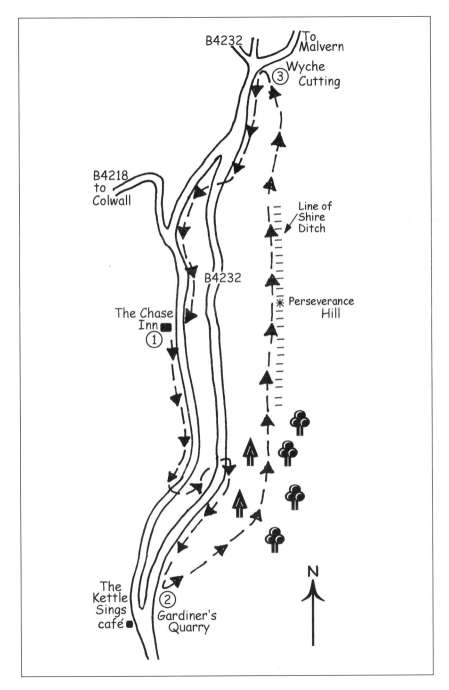

Looking north along the Malvern ridge

has recently been named Jubilee Hill, in honour of Queen Elizabeth. From here the route ahead is very clear, dropping down to a hollow and then up again to the next knob along the ridge.

Continue along the well-worn path, with rocky outcrops in places. You are following the line of the Shire Ditch, or Red Earl's Dyke, thought to have been created by Gilbert de Clare who was in dispute with the Bishop of Hereford over the boundary of their land. From the next summit, Perseverance Hill at 325m (1,066 ft), you can see ahead to an even bigger hill, the Worcestershire Beacon, but we are not going so far today. Begin to descend gradually, as the path leads down to the Wyche Cutting – an ancient trackway.

3. Descend a few steps to the road and turn left, on the B4218 towards Colwall, passing the toilets. The road soon splits and you stay on the left fork for the moment, the B4232 towards Ledbury, along Jubilee Drive. At the far end of the car park cross over and take the path descending through a rough grassy patch towards the Colwall road. Just before reaching the road turn left along the track and follow this in front of the houses. This leads down to the road on the sharp bend to Colwall. Take the narrow left turn off this road, to walk along Chase Road for about 250 yards to return to the pub.

13 Hanley Swan
The Swan Inn

*A gentle walk across the wide rich plain of the River Severn, with
the steep Malvern Hills dominating the landscape two miles to our
west, takes us through cropfields and pastures. Sheep and cattle
will be watching as we pass, and horses may thunder by, on the
Ox Hill gallop.*

The ancient village of Hanley Swan with its mix of timber-framed
cottages and more modern housing has grown up at a crossroads.
The shop and pub sit at this focal point, and the village church of
St Gabriel is just 100 yards away. The Swan Inn has an idyllic
location, set alongside the green, across which is Swan Pool, where
ducks and moorhens live, and water lilies and tall yellow irises
thrive. Across the road from the pond is an old oak tree planted on
the green in 1863 to celebrate the marriage of the Prince of Wales,
later to become King Edward VII. Local legend says that this tree was
only a puny sapling, until a travelling circus came to the green. The

elephant was allowed too close to this small tree, and bit off its top. Since when, it has grown magnificently!

Parts of the Swan Inn are over 400 years old and the bull's head hanging on the wall of the restaurant area is a reminder that for a time this was a butcher's shop. Bar meals are served in one room and the other is a more formal restaurant. A wide choice of snacks and meals includes daily specials, offers for OAPs and children's meals as well as tempting home-made dishes such as lasagne and beef pies. The large garden is delightful on a summer's day, providing space for children, views of the green and occasional visits from the ducks wandering across from the pond, to join in your lunch. This tenanted pub gives a friendly welcome to walkers and offers a range of regular beers as well as rotated special guest beers. Opening times are 12 noon to 3 pm and 6 pm to 11 pm, with food served from 12 noon to 2 pm and 6.30 pm to 9 pm (no meals on Sunday or Monday evenings). Telephone: 01684 310639.

- **HOW TO GET THERE:** Hanley Swan is reached along the B4211 and then the B4209 from Upton upon Severn, or the B4208 or B4209 from Malvern.
- **PARKING:** Park at the pub (with permission of course) or the slip road alongside the green.
- **LENGTH OF THE WALK:** 4 miles. Map: OS Explorer 190 Malvern Hills and Bredon Hill (GR 813429).

THE WALK

1. Start from the little slip road by the Swan, and walk towards Upton. After passing a few houses, reach a milestone, 3 miles to Upton, and a narrow surfaced track going left. Turn here, following the footpath sign. The surfaced track soon becomes a green track between hedges, and you say goodbye to traffic. Views to the left look over houses of Hanley Swan to the hills beyond.

At the end of the large field go straight ahead over a stiled footbridge, along the left margin of the next field. Halfway along this field, where a footpath leads left over a stile, you may notice in the distance the Catholic church of Our Lady and St Alphonsis, built by the Hornyold family, an important Catholic landowning family whose home was in Blackmore Park. The church architect was Charles Hansom, brother of Joseph Hansom, of hansom cab fame.

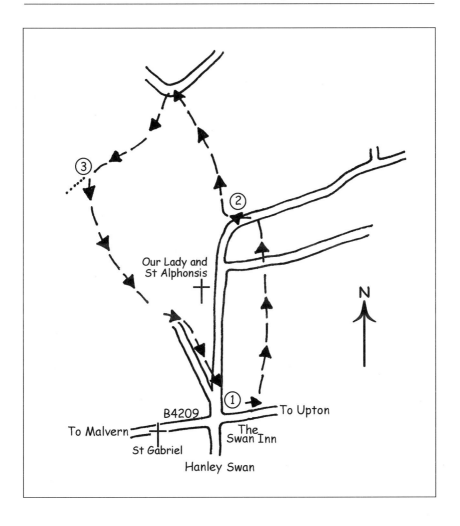

However, you keep straight ahead, and in the corner of the field, go left over a stile, and then immediately right, to continue more or less straight ahead, but now with the hedge on the right. After a few yards reach another stile and go straight on to another stile and footbridge to the narrow road.

Move a few yards right and then go left over a stile, more or less keeping straight ahead, with a hedge on the left. Cross a small field to a stile by a gate. The next field is quite large, and split by a stream, but head straight across to a stile you can see by the gate. The buildings over to the right are Blackmore End Farm.

2. At the road turn left, to walk along the grassy verge for 250 yards. Just before the road bends left, at the Hanley Swan sign on the left, go right, following the footpath sign. Go over the stile and walk along the field margin, with a narrow belt of trees to the left, and the Blackmore Park caravan site just through these trees. At the end of the field the path splits, and you keep straight ahead, over the stile and slightly left to follow the line of telegraph poles, to a stile on the far side of the field. The dramatic views left to the hills have changed again, and you are now looking at the Worcestershire Beacon (the highest point of the Malverns) and North Hill.

Cross the next small field, to another stile, still following the line of telegraph poles. Go over a stiled footbridge, and walk along the right side of the next field, with a big hedge on the right - covered with wild roses in season. Go over a stiled footbridge onto a narrow road, where you turn left. After about 30–40 yards, as the road bends right, go left along a stony track, which soon deteriorates to an earth track. Reach a gate, and keep ahead across a small paddock with farm barns to the left. Go on ahead through the wooden gate, and follow the footpath/bridleway sign, as you proceed along a grassy track between big hedges - a wonderful location for bird life. Reach a few muddy patches, and then begin to climb slightly.

3. As the path levels out, turn left over a stile and cross the narrow field, which contains a gallop for the local horses - which are numerous. You are on Ox Hill, which was formerly named Hawks Hill, and is now managed by the Malvern Hills Conservators.

On the other side of this field is another stile, and from here views of the southern end of the range can be seen to the right, and the caravan site down to the left. As you begin to descend, the walled garden and then a pond can be seen down to the left, with the caravan park beyond. This area is all part of the Hornyold estate.

Reach a stony drive, and keep straight ahead. Pass through the large iron gate and follow the grassy track along the edge of an open field, with yet more good views over to the hills.

Come onto a stony drive, passing Stable Farm to the left. Notice the bell tower with an unusual one-handed clock. The drive splits, the right turn passing the disused Army hospital camp site, but you keep straight ahead, soon to reach a 'Private Road' notice, footpath only - which is all you want. So just keep straight ahead, admiring the views and reach the village pond and your starting point in Hanley Swan.

14 Hanley Castle
The Three Kings

A gentle walk takes us past the ancient church to the site of the castle, where King John came for the hunting. In his day the landscape would not have been of crops and pastures, but of forest - the Malvern Chase. The long panoramic view of the Malvern range will not have changed, and remains as the ever present backcloth.

The village is centred round the church and pub where we begin our walk, but in ancient times there were strong links with the river. Part of the village is across the main road, the B4211, on the narrow Quay Lane leading down to the Severn. China clay used to come here by river, when Hanley Castle was noted for its pottery. The church of St Mary is of Saxon origin though rebuilt in Norman times. A section of the nave survives from the 13th century, but there was a major rebuild in the 14th century and again in the 19th. The tower is from the 17th century - and is of brick (built 1674). Timber-framed almshouses and school sit attractively alongside the church.

The earliest records of the school are from 1523 but it is almost certainly older than this.

The Three Kings is a beer drinkers' paradise, with a wide choice of beers – and a beer festival here each November. An award-winning free house, it serves traditional ales, including guest beers as well as beers from small independent breweries. Although beer is more important than food here, there is good home-cooked food with a choice of bar snacks as well as main course meals including grills.

The pub is situated on part of the Lechmere estate, which extends from their house alongside the Severn – and inside the church are Lechmere family memorials. The 15th century Three Kings is a very attractive, interesting and historical building – and in a delightful setting. At the end of the lane, it sits alongside the church and several houses, with magnificent colourful gardens. There are two small bars in what was the original pub, but now more space and dining area are available in the extension, which was formerly a separate cottage (black and white). Flagstone floors, old furniture and a huge inglenook fireplace are part of the interior décor in this old inn which has been run by the Roberts family since 1911. It is open from 11 am to 3 pm and 7 pm to 11pm, and occasionally has live music. Food is served 12 noon to 2.30 pm and in the evening by arrangement. Bed and breakfast accommodation is available. Telephone: 01684 592686.

- **HOW TO GET THERE:** Hanley Castle is just off the Upton upon Severn to Worcester road, B4211/B4244, one mile north of Upton.
- **PARKING:** There is parking adjacent to the pub.
- **LENGTH OF THE WALK:** 4 miles. Map: OS Explorer 190 Malvern Hills and Bredon Hill (GR 839420).

THE WALK

1. Eventually you have to leave the pub and go on your walk, but we will keep it short. From the pub and the large cedar tree, walk through the gate into the churchyard, passing to the left of the war memorial (which contains the remnants of an ancient cross) and then left of the church, close to the east wall. The church is unusual being part stone and part brick, and has a large clock on the brick tower. Go through an old iron kissing gate and into a field, walking along the right margin by the hedge. After a right bend the path soon divides; go left here. Still following the same field boundary, look for

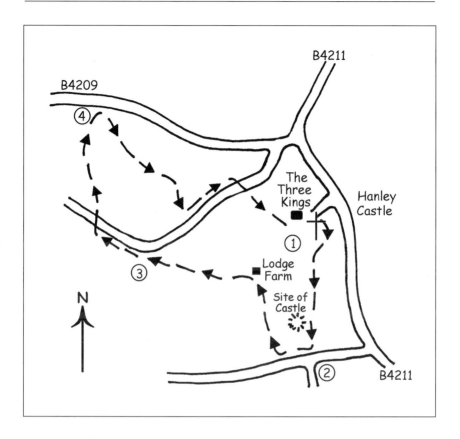

a path to the right, where you turn, to the old iron kissing gate 10 yards away. Go on to a stile, cross over the small stream (Pool Brook) and then another stile by an iron gate. After a further 20 yards the path divides. Your route is left over the stile, but first go ahead between the old stone gateposts, and then left to walk past the large Wellingtonia tree to visit the castle mound, the site of King John's castle.

The castle was built as a hunting lodge for King John who was a regular visitor to this area. He stayed at the castle several times during 1209–1213, and is buried in Worcester Cathedral. Only a ditch and the mound remain now, but after the time of King John it was used by the Earls of Warwick and the Duke of Gloucester (who became Richard III) and was probably the centre of the administration for the Malvern Chase. After it decayed some of the stones were used for building the bridge at Upton (now replaced by a more modern bridge).

The Three Kings pub sign

Once over the stile walk along the track on an embankment, with a marshy area of the old moat to the right, and a low area with Pool Brook to the left. Reach a stile by a gate, pass the modernised old mill, and go straight ahead through the garden and follow the driveway to come out on the narrow road.

2. Turn right. Ignore the left turn to Clive's Farm but continue straight along the road, for about 100 yards. Turn right at the footpath sign, to go over the stile by an old iron gate, and follow the track. This leads across an open meadow, and on through an open gate, between a hedge on the left and a fence on the right, to reach an iron gate. Go straight on, across the open field, towards the house ahead, which is Lodge Farm.

At the buildings, and the large fir tree in the corner of the garden, turn left to walk alongside the hedge on your right. Go on through an iron kissing gate and continue along the edge of the next field, to reach a meeting point of three paths. Stay close to the left margin of the field, but head across towards a stile near the trees to the left of the large house - Gilbert's End Farm.

3. At a stile by a gate, go onto the road and turn left, with the buildings on your right - notice the impressive tall chimneys of this handsome house. Follow the road for about 400 yards, and just before the 30 sign, turn right, following a footpath sign to a stile alongside a gate. Stay close to the left margin of the field, and at the end of the field, go through a gate and across the middle of the next field. Go over a stile and head towards the far right corner where there is a stile, over which you go and then immediately turn left, alongside the hedge. Stop at the next stile which is about 20 yards from the gate and the road.

4. Turn round here and walk back through the same field, but along the left margin now, to a smart new stile with a doggy opening. Beyond here turn left and find the next stile in the left corner. Go over this and along the left side of a large field. When the hedge ends continue straight ahead across this large field, bending slightly to the right to reach the hedge at the far side. Turn right along this field boundary until it turns left at a right angle bend, and then follow this hedge to the gate and out onto the road.

Turn left along this road for about 400 yards, passing over Pool Brook near the driveway to Lodge Farm. A few yards beyond where a footpath goes left, turn right to follow the path between hedge and fence. The hedge ends and you continue between fences, with good open views on both sides. Come to an iron kissing gate and enter the playing field of Hanley Castle school, and follow the right boundary to reach another gate and a short stretch of driveway to complete the circuit.

⓫ Newbridge Green
The Drum and Monkey

A flat walk along the Severn and through Upton, passing over farmland including the huge pasture area of the hams, often flooded in winter. At all times, either the Upton church spire or the Malvern Hills will be in view – or sometimes both.

Upton upon Severn is a throbbing small town popular with tourists in summer, especially caravanners and boaters. Its numerous pubs are an added attraction. The town is steeped in history, and a Town Walk pamphlet is available from the Tourist Information Centre. Upton grew because of the river and still has close links though in winter these may become too close – when it floods. The main road is occasionally blocked. It was an important crossing point as long ago as 1651 when a major battle in the Civil War took place here. A plaque commemorating Cromwell's visit to the town can be seen on the building opposite the statue of Admiral Tennant, which takes pride of place in the garden of the Pepperpot.

The main bar area of the Drum and Monkey dates from 1620 and part of an original wattle and daub wall can still be seen. The door leading to the Ladies is in an original outside wall. Additions in the 19th century contributed to today's light and spacious pub with comfortable eating areas, which include the Barn Restaurant. Snacks and a wide choice of freshly cooked meals are served at lunchtimes from 12 noon to 2 pm on Tuesday to Sunday and in the evenings from 6.30 pm to 9 pm on Monday to Saturday. This free house offers a wide range of beers, the real ales including Jennings Cocker Hoop and Marston's Pedigree – and there is a darts board. The delightful garden gives clear views to the Malvern Hills. A skittle alley, formerly a bakery, is also available here. Telephone: 01684 594705.

- **HOW TO GET THERE:** About a mile west of Upton upon Severn on the A4104 Ledbury-Upton road turn southwards on the B4211 towards Newbridge Green and Longdon.
- **PARKING:** There is ample parking at the pub, but several public car parks are to be found in Upton.
- **LENGTH OF THE WALK:** 5½ miles. Map: OS Explorer 190 Malvern Hills and Bredon Hill (GR 844392).

THE WALK

1. Cross the road and turn right for a few yards then go left down the country lane. Note that the house on the corner is called Cruck House – an indication of its architecture. The lane soon splits and you keep straight ahead (the lane going left is the return route). Follow this narrow surfaced road leading to Southend Farm. Keep ahead through the farmyard between buildings. The surfaced road has become a stony track. Bend left, with a brick wall on the right, and enjoy the wonderful view to Upton church spire. Follow a concrete drive for a few yards, as far as an iron gate on the right. Go through this gate and head across the large field, passing to the right of the lone oak tree in the middle. Reach a small bridge over a stream with a stile beyond. The footpath is now on top of an embankment which helps as a flood barrier but also serves as a footpath through flooded ground. The path leads through trees to reach a stile, then across a small field to another stile and the road.

2. Turn right. Walk through a modern housing development and as this road bends sharp left, go right along Buryend Road. Continue

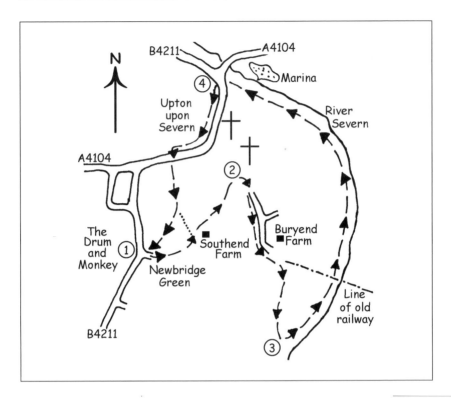

straight ahead past houses and into the farmyard. Beyond the buildings the drive bends left, but you keep straight ahead to pass through two large gates and into an open field, following the hedge on the right. Look for a stile to the right, which you cross but immediately turn left to follow the hedge. At the end of this field is a stile; keep straight ahead alongside a line of trees to reach a wooden stile set into a wire fence. Ahead is a huge field of the hams (the name derived from Anglo Saxon, referring to meadows close to the river). Head to the far side of this field to reach the river bank.

3. Turn left alongside the Severn to walk upstream, back into Upton. You are now on the Severn Way with its logo showing an old Severn Trow. At the end of the first field is a stile, and then a double stile, where the embankment of the old railway comes from the left. It was constructed on an embankment to keep it above flood level. This was the old bridging point but no bridge remains. Continuing alongside the river, pass the Severn Trent Water plant, and as you approach the first buildings of Upton you will see the entrance to the Upton Marina. From the river bank you go over a couple of stiles then continue along a narrow road. Several grand houses are on the left – notably Old Walls, Severn House and the Malt House, the Georgian house with lovely gardens seen through the iron gate. At the Swan fork right to stay close to the river, and the bridge comes into sight – as well as large pleasure boats on the river.

4. Turn left at the King's Head, one of a fine choice of pubs in this busy and popular tourist town. Notice in the wall to the right the three markers to show flood levels in 1852, 1886 and 1947. At the main road, where the Tourist Information Centre is on the corner keep straight ahead along the main shopping street. But first, look at several features of interest to the right. On the corner is the war memorial, with sun dials at the top. In the garden, formerly the nave of the church, is the bust of Admiral Sir William Tennant (senior naval officer at Dunkirk). The Pepperpot, formerly the tower of the parish church, now houses the Heritage Centre.

Walk straight on through the town, and continue past the present church. The graceful spire is easily seen from miles around, including from the top of the Malvern Hills.

Leaving Upton on the A4104 reach a right bend, where you may notice a remnant of old road. Just beyond here, cross over the main road to turn left along a track, signed to Newbridge Green. Walk through the gate alongside The Lodge, and follow this grassy drive for about 300 yards then look for a stile going to the right. Go over here and turn immediately left to follow the hedge. Reach a pair of stiles and keep straight ahead to the hedge where you bend right. With the hedge and a stream bed on your left, walk along this field boundary to reach a gate and then follow the track. Just before reaching the large barn a stile on the left takes you onto a grassy path alongside some apple trees and poplars, then at the next stile you rejoin the farm track. Pass delightful modernised farm buildings before reaching the narrow road, which leads to a larger road where you turn right, back to the Drum and Monkey.

⑯ Wynds Point
The Malvern Hills Hotel

Industry and history are themes of this walk which takes us past (and into) a quarry, to the remnants of an old Benedictine priory and then visits the burial place of one of Malvern's most famous residents, Edward Elgar. Incidentally we pass through scenery with glorious views.

Wynds Point is where the main Malvern to Ledbury road cuts through a gap to cross the Malvern ridge. Below this point is Little Malvern which sits on the lower slopes of the hills. Little Malvern is only a tiny hamlet, consisting of a church, farm and Little Malvern Court. Little Malvern Priory dates from the 12th century, and the only remaining part of this former monastery is Priors Hall, now part of the Court, the home of the Berington family for centuries. The adjacent St Giles was the church of the Benedictine priory.

The Malvern Hills Hotel was formerly known as the British Camp Hotel, and the original building is at least 500 years old. The pub is open for drinks all day and offers several beers, including Dorothy Goodbody's, and an extensive choice of wines. A wide range of food is served from 12 noon to 2.15 pm and 6.30 pm to 9 pm; a set menu is always available and additions are listed on a board. There is ample room in the oak panelled bar, and also a large restaurant. The patio gives views over Herefordshire into Wales and the Black Mountains. Pool, darts and games machines are to be found in the downstairs bar. Children and dogs are welcome. En-suite accommodation may tempt you to stay longer. Telephone: 01684 540690.

- **HOW TO GET THERE:** The hotel is situated at Wynds Point, alongside the A449 Malvern–Ledbury road.
- **PARKING:** There is a car park at the hotel and a large public car park across the main road.
- **LENGTH OF THE WALK:** 5 miles. Map: OS Explorer 190 Malvern Hills and Bredon Hill (GR 763404).

THE WALK

1. Cross the road from the Malvern Hills Hotel and walk to the far end of the car park, beginning to go downhill into the woods. Follow the track, passing the 'No Wheeled Vehicles' notice and down to the reservoir and the house. Up to the right are the embankments of the British Camp, and it is on this slope that heather grows, the only place on the Malverns.

The surfaced track ends at the house but you keep straight ahead and descend quite steeply on a concrete track with gaps where greenery can grow - very eco friendly. Go downhill into the woods, with a stream joining on the right. Where it turns left, you go left off the track, onto a narrow and rocky path, still in the heart of the woods, with the stream on your right and a stone wall on your left.

Carry on descending through these beautiful woods, to reach a gate, where you go straight across a small field, with the farm to your right and views of Little Malvern Priory to the left.

2. At the stile turn left along the farm track. You already have good views over to the right, but there is much better to come. Continue along this concrete track to reach a lily pond and then colourful gardens and a house on the right. When you reach the road you are turning left, but first go right for a few yards to pass the old farm complex on the left, and on the right is the entrance to Little

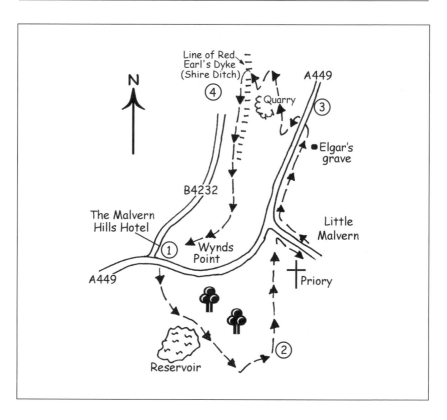

Malvern Court, which is sometimes open to the public, telephone: 01684 892988. Next door is Little Malvern church.

Retrace your steps now, walking uphill along the road, to reach a major road, where you turn right towards Malvern and Worcester. In the churchyard of the Roman Catholic parish church of St Wulstan, 200 yards along on the right you will find the Elgar family graves. An information plaque gives a little information but also quotes the Elgar remark of 1904: 'Music is in the air all around you, just take as much as you want.' Like other churches it has been built of local granite, but with the softer Cotswold limestone used for windows and door surrounds. At the main door there are three pillars of new red sandstone, the local rock of the Worcestershire Plain to the east.

3. Back on the road, pass the antique shop where a pine Amerindian is guarding the door. Take the left fork towards Holy Well. Not that you are going as far as Holy Well, instead after 30 yards, turn sharp left on the broad track leading uphill into the woods. This is the first part of the climb up to the ridge top, so take your time, and enjoy the birds and flowers in these woods. Like so many paths on the Malverns, even in wet weather this one is quite firm and dry.

At a major cross paths, turn sharp right, still climbing slightly before levelling off – as the amazing views open up to the right – and there are occasional benches where you can pause to admire these views. Walk on to the opening of the old Berington Quarry, where vegetation is covering part of the rocky slopes, with grasses and even trees. Most colourful is a lone rhododendron and many valerian, tough plants which seem to grow well even in very poor soil.

Your path soon begins to climb again, the second part of the climb to the ridge top – and the views become even better, or certainly different. The path begins to bend left, as you walk along the side of a steep valley down to your right. Just before a wooden bench, which offers clear views down the valley, turn sharp left off the main path, onto a narrow path to continue the climb.

4. Emerge from the trees on to the grassy ridge top, where the climate is different and another layer of clothing will be required. You are at a low point on the ridge, and ahead of you, looking north, is the steep climb to Pinnacle Hill, but you turn left to walk south, passing a boundary stone. If you had thought the views over Worcestershire were splendid, rural and often very green, from here the views west over Herefordshire into Wales are even more rural and greener.

The path south splits, with a choice of the ridge top or a gentle descent, but if you follow the broad path as it gently declines, you still have the wonderful views to the British Camp on the next beacon to the south. The path leads gently down into a car park, where a notice tells you that this has been the Easy Access Trail. Leave at the far left end of the car park to walk on past the left side of the house, and climb slightly up to a clear horizontal path where you turn right to reach four seats with a memorial plaque to Sir Barry Jackson (1879–1961), who founded Birmingham Repertory Theatre and helped to create the annual Malvern Festival in 1929. From here is one of the best views looking north along the ridge. Carry on along this path to descend to the road where you turn left to return to the Malvern Hills Hotel.

⑰ Chance's Pitch
The Wellington Inn

An old Iron Age fort dating from 400 BC tops the Herefordshire Beacon which rises to 339m (1,112 ft) - and is known locally as British Camp. We complete a circuit round this hill as well as exploring the woods clothing much of the east side. The pub itself is set alongside farm fields where we start and finish this invigorating and quite energetic walk.

The Wellington Inn dates back more than a century and the original part still retains some low beams - so mind your head if you are a six footer. Extensions have enlarged this attractive pub and the former skittle alley has been converted into a restaurant or function room with its own bar, with windows looking out across hills and woodland towards Ledbury. The garden also enjoys magnificent views. This privately owned free house serves real ales, Ruddles Best Bitter and Morland Old Speckled Hen, and holds an excellent selection of wines. The menu is outstanding with a range of full meals and snacks, as well as daily specials on the board. A feature of the Wellington is its Italian fare, thanks to the Italian chef. Home-made sweets are another great attraction. How about chocolate mousse with cointreau cream! Opening hours are 11.30 am to 2.30 pm and 6.30 pm onwards. Food is available every lunchtime – and every evening except Sunday, when the renowned Sunday lunch extends well into the afternoon. Telephone: 01684 540269.

- **HOW TO GET THERE:** The Wellington Inn will be found 3 miles east of Ledbury on the south side of the main Ledbury–Malvern road, the A449.
- **PARKING:** There is ample car parking at the inn.
- **LENGTH OF THE WALK:** 7 miles. Map: OS Explorer 190 Malvern Hills and Bredon Hill (GR 743399).

THE WALK

1. From the pub turn right along the road for about 100 yards to a stile on the right. Cross a small field to a track and bear left into the next field. The path leads through the middle of this field, over a stiled footbridge, and then through two more fields up to a stile into the woods. Notice Ockeridge Farm to the left, with the British Camp beyond, showing its stepped silhouette. Up the slope through the trees you reach a stony track and turn left.

2. Climbing slightly, stroll along this track on the top of the Ridgeway, a hill of Wenlock limestone used as an old route, possibly a saltway in the past. The track splits and you fork right, leaving the stony track for a muddy and possibly damp route. Pass open fields sloping down to the right, to Netherton Farm, with the Eastnor Obelisk in view beyond. Reach a recently cleared area, and then the track splits three ways. Take the middle option and keep straight ahead to reach a bigger track.

3. Turn left here and immediately a steep track goes off to your right - ignore it. Climb steadily along the major track, and just before it begins to descend, fork right, onto the Worcestershire Way, to follow the pear sign.

4. Reach the road and Wynds Point is not far to the right. But because of no footpath and possible traffic problems, walkers are encouraged to turn left along the road for about 30 yards and then go right, still on the Worcestershire Way. Follow the drive past a house and along the track, until it bends to the right. Go left here,

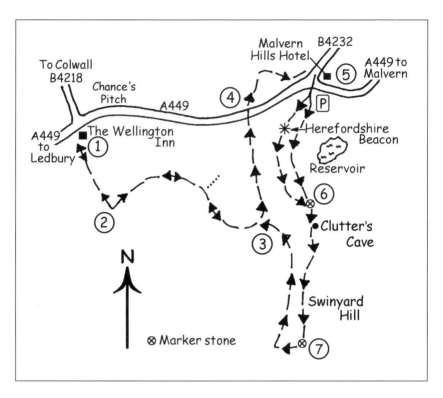

through old coppiced woodland. Leave the woods over a stile and cross the field to a point where paths divide. You need to turn right towards British Camp and the car park. After a few yards go over a stile, and the climb begins through woods - accompanied by a rich smell of garlic (ramsons). At the road, opposite the Malvern Hills Hotel, turn right to cross over the main road, to the car park.

5. There are two possible routes from here. EITHER take the first path on the right for the top of the Herefordshire Beacon. This is a steep climb, but worth every gasp. Once at the beacon just walk south along the ridge top and descend steeply to rejoin the alternative route at point 6. OR, to avoid the steep climb, a further 30 yards into the car park there is another path on the right, and this gives a more gentle ascent. A broad gravelled path rises steadily into the trees, but soon splits, and you keep straight ahead. Emerge from the trees to enjoy wonderful views left down to the reservoir and across the plain towards the Cotswolds. Amongst the local bird life, keep looking for a wheatear, with its white rump flashing as it flies

Looking towards Worcestershire Beacon

away. Also on this slope is the only heather to be seen on the Malverns. The broad path leads to a round guidestone with direction markers.

6. From the guidestone go straight ahead towards Giant's Cave and Pink Cottage, but first look a few yards to the left where the Shire Ditch can be seen (see also Walk 12). Beyond the ditch is Broad Down where a flock of sheep has been reintroduced by the Conservators to help control the growth of scrub. Follow the narrow path to the Giant's Cave, a manmade hollow in the rocks, possibly used by a hermit or a shepherd – and not easily created out of these hard rocks! Continue straight on, to descend to a hollow with a meeting point of several paths. This is Silurian Gap, named after the rocks of Silurian age (about 425 million years ago) which outcrop near here.

Keep straight ahead and along to the top of Swinyard Hill, where there are more views of Herefordshire and Wales to the right, with the Eastnor Obelisk ahead, and Castlemorton Common down to the left. After the highest point of Swinyard, you begin to descend.

7. At the next round marker stone, go right towards Midsummer Hill and the obelisk – not that we are going to either. Look out for wild flowers including the small bright yellow tormentil which thrives in acidic soils, but also wild thyme, and the tall yellow great mullein. A delightful book has been written by Keith Barnett about the flowers of the Malvern Hills - available in local bookshops.

Go down into the trees to reach a broad clear track, pitted by wheel tracks, where you turn right - look out for Range Rovers which are driven around in these woods. You are now on the Worcestershire Way again, shown by a yellow arrow and a pear logo. Swinyard Hill is up to the right, and woods extend to the left, beyond a wire fence. Descend slightly, and at the bottom of the slope a track comes up to join you from the left. After a few more yards reach a gate on your track, with a stile alongside. To the left here is a covered reservoir, and in a small fenced area to the right is Walms Well, probably used by the Iron Age inhabitants.

Pass over the stile to the left of the gate, and climb up to the first left turn (point 3). Turn down here - now retracing your steps as you came up here in the early part of the walk. Go back through the recently cleared patch, bear left alongside the open fields. When the track divides fork left and come onto the stony Ridgeway track and continue back towards the pub. In this stretch of woodland I always seem to be lucky enough to see a buzzard as there are a few pairs nesting near here. You may be lucky too! They lazily float if disturbed from their perch on a branch above. About $\frac{1}{2}$ mile along this track look for the marker post (point 2) where you turn right. Descend to the edge of the wood and cross the three fields to return to the Wellington.

⑱ Wellington Heath
The Farmers Arms

From Ledbury 25.8.08

Wellington Heath is hidden in a secluded valley with hills and woods all around, and fields of grazing sheep, cows and horses. Horse riding is very popular with local residents. Our walk takes us through woods, across pastures, into Coddington village and up to the top of Oyster Hill before descending through Hope End Estate, where Elizabeth Barrett lived for 23 years before eloping with Robert Browning.

Wellington Heath is a long, well-kept village with a ribbon of houses lining the narrow road. Trees and shrubs give a rural atmosphere, so that it truly merges with the surrounding countryside.

Set in this Area of Outstanding Natural Beauty, a section of the wooden-beamed Farmers Arms inn is believed to date from Tudor times. Formerly a farmhouse (with hams hanging from the beams), then a cider house, it became a more traditional pub in the 1950s. It is part of the Enterprise Inns group, serving good local ciders but also with a variety of beers, including a different guest beer each week. The Cowshed and the Orchard provide extra space for tables, while the terrace and garden are ready for good weather. The large eating area and car park are both signs of popularity, richly deserved as there is a wide choice of excellent food, and always extra daily specials. Two specially tempting items on my last visit were the home-made garlic and mushroom bake, and the Farmer's Hog Roast, a rack of pork with crispy crackling. The opening hours are 12 noon to 3 pm and 6 pm to 11 pm daily, with food always available, including a children's menu. Profound sayings and quotes are dotted around the walls and close to the bar is one of my favourites: 'Let us have wine and women, mirth and laughter, Sermons and soda water the day after' (Byron). The Gents is called the Cowmen, and the Milkmaids is the Ladies. Telephone: 01531 632010.

- **HOW TO GET THERE:** Leave Ledbury on the Bromyard road (B4214) and after ½ mile turn right to Wellington Heath. At the top of the hill turn sharp right and follow this narrow road. When the road divides take the right fork, which leads to the pub.
- **PARKING:** The Farmers Arms has a large car park.
- **LENGTH OF THE WALK:** 5 miles. Map: OS Explorer 190 Malvern Hills and Bredon Hill (GR 712403).

THE WALK

1. Leave the car park and turn left along the road, The Common, and climb steadily between houses. At the top is a T-junction and you turn right for about 30 yards before turning left at the footpath sign. Go over the stile alongside the large wooden gate, and follow the clear track, with woods on the right and open field on the left. The track descends steadily, and when it levels it forks; go left here to continue descending through Raven Hill Wood. The path leads to a stile on the edge of the woods and once over this you turn left to follow the hedge – still going downhill. As it levels off, bend over to the right to a gate in the hedge and go straight across the next field. Aim towards the gate clearly seen across the field but pass to the left of it alongside a hedge on your right, to reach a stile by a gate. Move slightly away from the hedge on your right, and over the stile at the far side of this next field. The buildings of Woofields Farm can be seen and Coddington church with its broach spire is ahead to the right. Cross this field to the point where the hedge turns at a right angle.

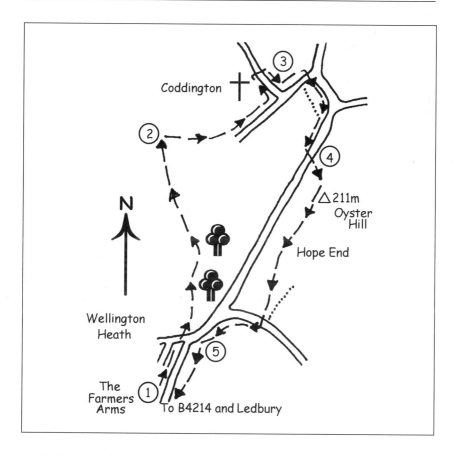

2. Turn right to follow the hedge, on your left. Continue to the stile, beyond which is the farm drive. Pause and look around at this point as there is almost certain to be a buzzard floating overhead.

Large barns are to the right, also modernised buildings with a clock tower, but you turn left to follow this narrow road. Pass a small pond and then reach Coddington Vineyard - well worth a visit! Continue along the road, climbing slightly, and at the road junction turn left to visit Coddington village and church. Around the church are several old buildings, including the delightful black and white Church Farm, the Old Rectory and the former village school. The stone church of All Saints is surrounded by a well-maintained churchyard from which there are excellent views across to Hay-on-Wye.

3. Retrace your steps along the narrow country lane to the road junction and fork left. Follow this narrow road to the junction and

The view to the British Camp

fork right, signed to Wellington Heath. Great views to the Malvern Hills open up through a gap in the hedge at this junction. The bare tops of the Malverns can be seen, with North Hill three peaks from the left, and then Sugar Loaf and the Worcestershire Beacon next moving to the right. The line of houses at West Malvern can be seen stretching out along the hillside. Walking along the road, climbing slightly, ignore the left turn and continue straight ahead, now climbing steadily.

4. When the road bends slightly right and begins to go downhill, fork left along a track with a public footpath sign. The track immediately divides and you fork right, to walk along to a large iron gate. Shortly beyond this gate the track divides and you fork right again, passing a few lone trees, and then climb onto the open hillside. The triangulation point is not at the top of Oyster Hill, possibly because the summit was densely covered by trees when the survey work was done. Walk on beyond the trig point at 211m (692 ft) and the adjacent seat, with commanding views to the west, including much of Shropshire (Clee Hills with its radar equipment) and into Wales. Gradually begin the descent, and soon reach a stile, then continue along a path between wire fences, with trees on the

right and open grassland to the left. Looking left you will see a grassy dry valley; 'hope' is Old English for a dry valley, and it was in this secluded place, on the Hope End Estate, that Mr Barrett built his rather grandiose Islamic-style house, with turrets and minarets, having bought the estate in 1809. This house was burned down in 1910, with only the stables remaining, but the modern replacement is still hidden away in this very quiet valley.

Walk on, following the clear path through the parkland, and to the left can be seen part of the old stable block. Reach another stile and go on into the open grassland area, and to the left are the walled garden and modern housing. As you proceed the path gently slopes down through beautiful parkland to a stile by the lodge house where the main drive leads up to Hope End House. Reaching the road, turn right. Pass the sign for the beginning of Wellington Heath and come to a road junction where you go left towards Bosbury and Ledbury.

5. Just before the first house on the left there is a car park for the stables and you turn left here to go over a stile, then along the right side of a small paddock to a stile and along the right margin of a field. There are good views across left to the Herefordshire Beacon. At the end of this field go over a stile and reach a track which you follow gradually downhill, passing houses on the left. At the last house, where the track ends, go right on to a grassy path sloping downhill to reach the road. Turn right to reach the end of The Common and the Farmers Arms.

⑲ Castlemorton
The Robin Hood

Just a short distance along the country lane opposite the pub lies unbeatable scenery on open common and the hills ahead. The views are spectacular and in summer the biggest noises will be the bird song and sheep with their lambs. Our circuit takes us to the Iron Age fort on Midsummer Hill, extending our views into Herefordshire and Wales, and then through Hollybush and back to the Robin Hood via the lovely Mill Pond. Much of the route is on common land, where visitors have freedom to roam and where some local residents have commoners' rights to graze their animals. History tells us that these small remnants of open land were part of the Royal Chase extending from the Malvern Hills to the River Severn, designated originally by William the Conqueror.

Parts of the Robin Hood date from the 15th and possibly even the 14th century. There are no bows and arrows in evidence now, unlike in medieval times, when this area was part of the Chase, a royal hunting ground. The old black and white building has had recent extensions, and there is also ample space in the garden. The pub motto is 'we do not serve fast food here, but we serve good food as fast as we can'. Excellent home-cooked dishes on the regular menu are enhanced with a few specials on the board, and you can treat yourself from the mouthwatering selection of sweets and coffees. Food is served from 12 noon to 2 pm and every evening (except Tuesday) from 7 pm to 9.30 pm.

One of the Punch Taverns, beers available include Boddington, Tetley and Bass, as well as lagers, Guinness on draft, and local Stowford cider from across the hills at Weston's in Much Marcle. Always offering a friendly welcome, the pub has a warming fire in cold weather, a well-used darts board, and a touring caravan site at the rear. Telephone: 01684 833212.

- **HOW TO GET THERE:** The Robin Hood is located on the B4208 between Welland and Castlemorton village, and easily reached via the A4104 from Malvern or Upton upon Severn.
- **PARKING:** There is ample parking space at the pub.
- **LENGTH OF THE WALK:** 6 miles. Map: OS Explorer 190 Malvern Hills and Bredon Hill (GR 786380).

THE WALK

NB: The walking is mostly gentle, though a steep descent from Midsummer Hill can be slippery in wet weather and good walking shoes or boots are advisable.

1. Cross the road from the Robin Hood to walk along New Road, a narrow country lane. Pass a few houses but already the rural views are taking over. Ignore a right turn and soon reach another junction where you ignore the left turn. The narrow road begins to climb slightly up to the common, with Swinyard Hill as the backcloth in the distance. Farm buildings and a small pond are on the left as you reach the open common. Turn left at a T-junction where a George VI post box is attached to a telegraph pole.

Follow the line of the road as you begin to climb gently. Nature lovers can enjoy the black poplar trees near two small ponds which are home to a population of newts. The hills ahead are Swinyard with a treeless upper section, then to the left is the well-wooded Midsummer Hill. Cast your eyes further left to the most southerly of the Malverns, Ragged Stone Hill and finally Chase End Hill.

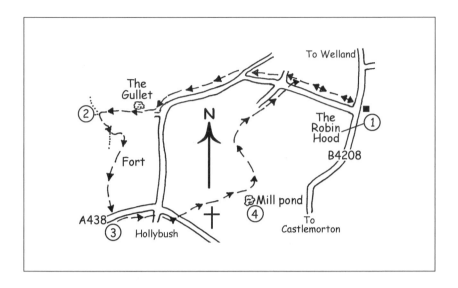

After reaching a parking area on the right, the road splits. Fork left and begin to descend. At the bottom of the slope cross a stream and, as the road bends left, fork right off the road onto the path into woods. Climb up to a major track and turn right. In these woods look out for a tree creeper, a little brown mouse-like bird working its way up trees, searching for insects in the bark.

Continue along this track, passing the Gullet Quarry on the right. Quarrying ceased here in 1977, and the quarry floor is now filled by a lake. Tempting for swimming on a hot summer day, but potentially very dangerous; warning notices have been placed here by the Conservators. The far side of the quarry shows a remarkable geological unconformity, with Pre-Cambrian rocks of 600 million years age at the bottom, but much younger Silurian rocks (a mere 425 million) above. A great location for geology students – and also for jackdaws which nest on the rocky slopes. Follow the gravel track as it climbs steadily through the woods, and at the top reach a major cross paths and the gate leading into Eastnor Park.

2. Turn left just before this gate, following the sign for the Worcestershire Way South. The stony track climbs steadily, passing a lone house on the left. Just beyond the driveway to this house, take the first left turn and follow the grassy path, with a hedge on the left and bracken on the right. Climb up and soon bend right, passing through an embankment of the former Iron Age hill fort. Continue

The ridge top from Swinyard Hill

on up to the small shelter at the top of the hill. A memorial plaque says that this area was given to the National Trust in 1923 in memory of Captain Ronald Somers Cocks MC - from the Eastnor family.

Continue straight ahead from the summit, admiring breathtaking views to right and left, including Eastnor Castle, looking like a toy fort. Ragged Stone Hill is straight ahead, and May Hill, beyond the Malvern ridge, with its distinctive clump of trees can also be seen in the distance. Descend quite steeply through the embankment of the old fort, and the woods, following a clear path. It can be quite slippery so take great care. Reach the grassy slope and go down to the car parking area.

3. Turn left along the road, to walk downhill, passing old thatched cottages with lovingly tended gardens on the right, then the Hollybush Pottery, as you re-enter Worcestershire. The entrance to the huge quarry is on the left, and after a few more houses you reach the crossroads where narrow roads go right and left. Next is the Hollybush Church Room dated 1915, and you continue along the verge for about 200 yards to reach the common. Fork left to follow the path on the left side of the common, passing between a large stone house with stable block on the left and a tiny cottage on the right. Hollybush church is to the right here if you wish to make a short detour.

Distant views open up ahead across the plain towards Bredon Hill, as the path begins to descend to Mill Pond. Popular with fishermen and picnickers, the pond is also home to many ducks, geese, coots and moorhens. On busy days an ice cream van visits, and there are a few seats if you are in need of a rest. A notice board gives information about the pond and this area. The pool was created in the late 19th century, and there was a working mill here, now demolished, but in use for grinding corn until 1943.

4. Walk to the left of the pond, then turn left alongside the hedge which separates the common from the farmed fields. Amongst the wealth of bird life you might be lucky enough to see on the commons is the smart and dapper stonechat, which has the decency to sing from the top of a gorse bush to enable bird watchers to see it clearly. Also quite thoughtful are yellowhammers and linnets, but less amenable are the chiffchaffs and willow warblers which are generally hidden. In the sky above there may be skylarks and pipits, showing off their ability to fly and sing at the same time. It is difficult to imagine a more beautiful spot on a summer afternoon.

As the path approaches houses, turn right before the house on the right, and follow the edge of the common alongside the gravel drive. Continue along this drive to reach a real, though still very narrow, road. Pass a few fairly isolated houses and after climbing a slight hill to Chandler's Farm, with its smart Malvern stone wall, reach the road junction you saw earlier. Turn right here and follow the road to return to the Robin Hood.

20 Birtsmorton
The Farmers Arms

A lovely walk round the country lanes, bordered by hedges rich in bird life and heavy with fruits and berries in season. A view of the hills is ever-present. We can admire Birtsmorton Court and church, before walking back across the fields.

The ancient settlement of Birtsmorton has evolved along the narrow lanes between the A438 and B4208. Buildings are in two locations, near the pub in Birts Street, and then a mile away at Birtsmorton Court and the church, which dates from about 1200. The Court has Norman foundations and is a moated medieval manor house with 12th century water channels. Its boom period was in the 15th and 16th centuries whilst owned by the Nanfans, courtiers of the Tudor kings. The magnificent gardens also probably date from the 16th century but had decayed and have been restored wonderfully during the last 30 or so years.

The Farmers Arms is a 16th century building with some fragments probably from 1480. This black and white pub is a free house serving

Hook Norton and Courage beers and Weston's ciders. Several old beams have survived though some changes have been made to make the interior more spacious. There is outside seating at the front of the pub. Food is served from 12 noon to 2 pm and 6 pm to 9.30 pm and the hours of opening vary slightly with the seasons. Everything is home cooked and a noted speciality is the unique Herefordshire minced beef pie. It is thought that the pub was a drovers' stop between Wales and London, and possibly on a stagecoach route. Local inhabitants believe that highwaymen were based in nearby Castlemorton village. Telephone: 01684 833308.

- **HOW TO GET THERE:** Take the B4208 which links the A438 to the A4104. Look carefully for the narrow left turn signed eastwards to Birtsmorton.
- **PARKING:** There is a car park at the pub.
- **LENGTH OF THE WALK:** 3½ miles. Map: OS Explorer 190 Malvern Hills and Bredon Hill (GR 790363).

THE WALK

1. From the pub door turn left and then left again along the narrow country lane, leaving the ancient Little Tudor, a black and white cottage, on the right. Walk along the road, and soon pass the 30 sign. After a straight stretch pass a couple of houses on a winding stretch of road.

2. When the road divides, fork right towards Rye Street. Just before reaching The Coach House and The Old Rectory on the left, turn left. Go through the big iron gate, and head straight across the large field, in an easterly direction. Cross this prairie-like field, heading towards the left hand end of the prominent white barn. Continue alongside the barn and follow the track to reach the road. Your onward route is to the left, but first go right – the reason for walking to this point. A few yards to the right is the fine stone church of Birtsmorton, set in a tidy churchyard with several fine coniferous trees. The first church on this site was built about 1180 but it was of wood and burned down. The present church dates from about 1300, and contains a stone tomb for the Nanfan family from the 15th century. The font is even older, from around 1100, but much of the church is more recent. The panels of the Ten Commandments were part of the reredos but were moved to their present position in 1877.

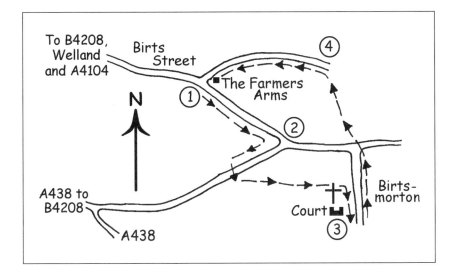

3. A little further along the road is the impressive driveway entrance to Birtsmorton Court and to have a better look at this incredible old building, walk on past the main entrance to a small bridge over a stream, from where there are good views through the trees. Even better is to continue a further few yards then turn right at the footpath sign and wander through the small gate along the path for 100 yards or so, to enjoy the view over the pond to the Court, with the Malvern Hills in the background. Catch a glimpse, and a small taster, of the gardens beyond the left hand end of the house.

After soaking up a bit of history, return to the road and turn left for the return journey to the pub. Follow the narrow road in a northerly direction to the T-junction and go straight across to the gate and the footpath sign. Walk along the right margin of this field to reach a stiled footbridge. Continue across the next field to another stile, then cross a third field on the right side of a lone oak tree to find another stiled footbridge in the hedge.

4. Go out onto the road and turn left. Pass a farm on the right and enjoy the views straight ahead to the peaked top of Ragged Stone Hill, with a little grass at the summit, though trees are gradually extending up the slopes. Miller's Court is on the right, followed by a small pond over which can be seen the spire of Castlemorton church. House martins will be flittering over the pond in the

Birtsmorton Court with the Malvern Hills beyond

summer months. Follow this country lane round to a T-junction and turn left, to pass a couple of semis on the right. Walk on past the Old Forge on the right – a listed house. You soon pass Bray's Farm on the left and arrive back at the Farmers Arms.